BEGINNER'S RACQUETBALL

by Jack Kramer

WORLD

World Publications, Inc.
Mountain View, California

Library of Congress Cataloging in Publication Data

Kramer, Jack, 1927 -
   Beginner's racquetball book.

   Includes index.
   1. Racquetball. I. Title.
GV1017.R3K7   796.34   78-64387
ISBN 0-89037-160-1

World Publications
Mountain View, CA

Acknowledgments

My thanks to John C. Stewart, Rick Partty, John Thomas and the owners of the Wallbanger Courts in Corte Madera, California for allowing to photograph on their premises, and to Bruce Radford for his modeling services. And gratitude to many of the players there that shared their knowledge of the game with me.

A special thanks to the U.S. Racquetball Association and National Racquetball Club for permission to reprint the Official Rules.

Contents

Introduction

I started playing racquetball a few years ago for sport and pleasure—not for competition. I wanted (and needed) a fitness program, and it struck me that since I played a lot of tennis and handball in my youth, racquetball might be the game for me. I checked with my doctor, and he said to try it moderately, and I did. I play it at my pace—never hard, never fast or furious. I am over 50 and know better.

Being a professional writer for the last twenty years, it dawned on me that since I enjoyed the game so much and saw others enjoying it, perhaps a book on racquetball for the beginner would be in great demand. I felt there were thousands of people like me out there who had not played a sport in some time, who wanted some exercise for body and mind.

Some 30 million people now play racquetball—this is an impressive testimonial for this sport. But it is well-deserved because racquetball makes you run, stretch, and think. It is an excellent way to keep the body in shape and help promote good cardiovascular health.

Racquetball does not have to be an expensive recreation (you can even rent racquets rather than buy), and the game can be played all year long at any time in most all cities. Thirty minutes of racquetball played twice a week gives the average person all the exercise he needs. In addition to the benefits of health and fitness, there is the reward of playing a sport well. And too, there is a good deal of social camaraderie in this sport.

The game can be played as you like it—moderately or intensely. I select opponents carefully and do so on a "Let's play and have some fun and fitness" basis—never by the "I can beat you" syndrome. This way, racquetball for me is an ideal way to get exercise and fun.

This book is written for all those many people who want to play the game for recreation and for sport and do it successfully. As I played, I relearned the game and wrote about it. I hope this information helps you play racquetball successfully.

Part

Preliminaries: What a Racquet!

1

Racquetball and You

The real origin of racquetball can probably be traced to the (unrecorded) origin of handball. The game does resemble handball in some instances. However, the records tell us that racquetball was directly derived from paddleball, a game that started about 1930 using wooden paddles. Tennis players of the 1920s realized they could improve their game by practicing on indoor handball courts in winter. A sort of paddle tennis emerged, and an avid athlete Earl Riskey, associated with the Department of Athletics at the University of Michigan in Ann Arbor, championed this tennis-handball concept.

In the 1930s, a shortened version of the tennis racquet made of wood appeared and the game of paddleball originated—a short wooden paddle instead of a racquet and a sponge rubber ball instead of a regulation tennis ball. So the true start of racquetball were these tennis players of the 1920s-30s.

Squash is a racquetball game played in an enclosed court with a 27-inch racquet and rubber ball. In this game the ball must be returned to the front wall above a line on the wall and below the out-of-court line without touching the floor.

Paddleball played with a 16-inch racquet can be played with one, three, or four walls in an enclosed court and, like squash, bears resemblance to racquetball.

WHO CAN PLAY

No matter whether racquetball had its start in squash or racquetball, it is a sport that almost anyone can play. I have seen youngsters of ten or eleven have their fling at it and I have seen oldsters in their fifties and sixties playing the game like twenty-year-olds. It all depends on you and your own physical condition. And certainly if you are over thirty-five, you should first have a physical checkup by a doctor to determine if racquetball is the sport for you, and if so, your limits in terms of exertion. No one can answer these questions for you except your doctor.

In essence, racquetball is a fast and furious game that benefits all parts of the body in varying degrees. You use your arms, legs, your whole body. It tones muscles, improves balance and agility. In the *Resident and Staff Physician*, reprinted in the *U.S. News and World Report*, April 4, 1977, it is in the top ten as a physical fitness activity (with handball and squash). It gives you stamina, muscular endurance, muscular strength, flexibility, and balance.

PHYSICAL FITNESS

Can you lose weight by playing racquetball? You sure can because you burn up about 360 calories per hour (as compared to 300 calories for swimming or cycling, for example). You will rarely see a heavy racquetball player.

Physical fitness is generally categorized in three ways: muscular, skeletal, and cardiovascular. The tone and strength of your muscles promoted by exercise is *muscular fitness. Skeletal fitness* is determined by the body's flexibility. *Cardiovascular fitness* refers to the strength and health of your heart and blood vessels and is perhaps the most important aspect of your general health.

Racquetball uses all your muscles because it keeps you moving and stretching. And it demands extra exertion on the cardiovascular system—heart and lungs. It is not a game to be taken lightly or played loosely because you use you whole body to get into the swing of racquetball.

So, if you are in good health, racquetball can do a great

deal to make you feel better both physically and emotionally. There is a very real feeling of well-being after playing a good game and your body will stay in shape longer and better because you are getting maximum exercise when you play racquetball. Ask your doctor.

SAFETY CONSIDERATIONS

As you start to play, you will have some aches and pains getting those muscles moving again. Never overdo—much better to play a half hour than an hour. Take it easy. Start slowly and gradually work into a routine your body can tolerate. Never jump into a game without warming up (more on this later) and never play more than your body tells you you should. There will be symptoms— a cramp, an ache, a pain. Pay heed to these signals.

If you have back trouble or any type of heart problem, or in fact any physical disorder, do not, and I repeat, *do not* play racquetball without checking with your physician first.

PLAYING THE GAME

It is said that it is not winning the game that counts, but how you play it. If you are thinking of a career in the sport, of course you would train and approach the game differently than the person who wants to use the game for exercise and sheer recreation. Almost every racquetball court center—and there are many throughout the United States—has an instructor. You will find courts listed in the yellow pages of your phone book, and if you want private or group instruction, the courts can give you the cost and other pertinent information.

Championships and competitions of all kinds are offered by local centers—there are dozens of them (too many to list here) and information is posted in these facilities. There are regional tournaments and championships on the state level and up-to-date information on these can be found in *National Racquetball Magazine* and other similar publications at the courts.

Play it as you will but do play—it is worth the time and effort and provides good physical exercise and the emotional pickup we all need from time to time.

2

Racquetball Equipment

If you have ever hit a ball against a wall with your hand, a bat, or a tennis racquet, you can play racquetball. Indeed, racquetball is similar in many respects to handball—just consider the racquet an extension of your hand. And the game also resembles tennis to some degree.

Racquetball is played on a standard handball court that measures 20 x 20 x 40 feet (see figure 2-1). The game is played within a four-wall court: a front and back wall and two side walls; the ceiling is also used. The court can be made of cement or prefabricated panels and glass, but more often it is wood. A minimum amount of equipment is required to play racquetball: a racquet, a ball, gym shoes and heavy socks, and some comfortable clothing, usually gym shorts and a T-shirt. Men may find an athletic supporter functional.

RACQUETS

The basic piece of equipment for racquetball is, of course, the racquet, so it is important to have a racquet that feels comfortable in your hand. The grip or feel of the racquet is important. There are several kinds of racquets; it pays to try them all before you make a final decision. Wooden-rimmed racquets are still available, but the heavy wooden rim can cause wood shots, which are not desirable. Wood racquets are usually shorter in length than those made of nonwood materials.

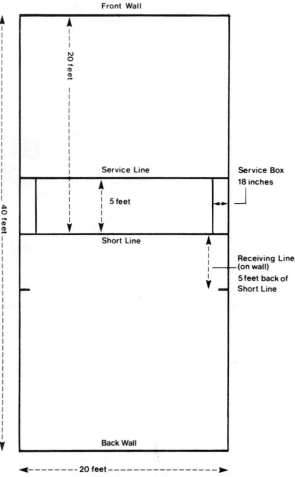

Fig. 2-1. Racquetball court dimensions

Plastic, fiberglass, or metal racquets get the nod these days, with plastic presently being the favorite of professionals. The plastic-rimmed racquet has great flexibility, giving somewhat upon ball contact so there is more snap back and thus more power. There is also better feel of the ball on the plastic racquet—more touch. Some people may, therefore, find that a plastic racquet gives them more control. On the other hand, plastic racquets are subject to more snapping or breaking than metal ones.

Metal-rimmed racquets—aluminum—wear well and seldom break. They can take more abuse than the plastic racquets, but they do not have as much give when the ball hits the strings.

Aluminum and fiberglass racquets—try before you buy

The length of the racquet is important. Official regulations state that the racquet head must not be wider than nine inches or longer than eleven inches. The maximum handle length cannot exceed seven inches. Thus the *maximum* size of the racquet is twenty-seven inches (9 plus 11 plus 7 inches). For non-official play there is an extra-long racquet; it is one inch longer (twenty-eight inches) than the maximum official length. This extra inch can be bad or good, depending upon your individual style of hitting the ball. Generally, the longer racquet is considered a disadvantage, because it can hamper wrist movement during ball contact and is generally harder to bring around on a stroke.

The choice of racquet material is up to you; do consider how any racquet feels in your hand. First try a racquet in your hand for feel, comfort, and general weight. Follow your instincts rather than someone else's advice.

Strings and Grips

The strings of the racquets are almost always made of nylon (catgut is rarely used today). The nylon is monofilament, unlike the multifilament (double string) used in tennis racquets. There are various grades of monofilament nylon: the clearer the better. Painted monofilaments may be inferior. Some nylon racquets are braided with red, blue, or other colored strings strictly for decorative purposes.

How tightly the racquet is strung—tension—can influence your game. Racquets are strung at 26 to 34 pounds (the 34-pound racquet having more tightness). The ideal string tension is about 28 to 30 pounds, neither too tight nor too loose. When considering tension, remember that it takes a few good games for the strings to settle in; in other words, the strings will loosen up about two to three pounds after a week or so of playing.

The grip, the part of the racquet you hold in your hand, may be covered with rubber or leather. Rubber may become wet and slippery, so usually you have to wear a glove. A rubber and cork handle has a good feel but can wear down. The leather grip is superior to the rubber one because it gives you less possibility of slippage. Or at least you can play somewhat longer without the racquet slipping or having to use a towel to wipe your hand. And real leather grips outlast rubber ones. The imitation leather grips feel sticky after you play awhile.

Grip size is also important. Grip sizes are small, medium, or large, or scaled into 1/8-inch increments. The 4-1/8 grip is generally the most popular, because it fits the average male and female player; children use a slightly smaller size. Always feel and test the grip before buying a racquet. And one warning: do not get a grip that is too large for you to handle. It is better to buy a smaller grip and then tape it to the right thickness.

THE BALL

The standard racquet ball is 2.5 inches in diameter, weighs 1.4 ounces, and is sold in cans, like tennis balls. There are several manufacturers of racquet balls; the only thing I can say about the various balls is that they are consistently inconsistent.

One ball from a two-ball can may jump like a startled grass-hopper, whereas the other ball may just plop like a shedded tear. Once you find a manufacturer who supplies the best uniformity of ball liveliness, stick with that brand.

CLOTHING

You can clothe yourself in some fancy sports gear—lovely pin-striped shorts, flashy T-shirts, and so on—but this is not necessary. If you are comfortable, you can play in pants. Generally, regulation gym shorts and a T-shirt are used, although many wear tennis garb, which is fine. Whatever clothing you select, be sure it is loose and comfortable.

You might want a warm-up suit for pre- and post-game play if you are subject to colds. Playing works up quite a sweat, and it is a good idea to cover up afterward. You do not need anything elaborate; a warm-up suit or jacket is fine.

Shoes and Socks

The kind of shoes you wear for racquetball can make the difference between a good game and a bad one. Proper fitting shoes are essential. Whichever brand of shoe you select (and there are many), it should be a thick sole with plenty of overall support. Racquetball requires a lot of pivoting and pushing off and shoes are the key. Thin-soled track shoes won't work, and neither will those old gym shoes.

Good basketball shoes are fine for racquetball. Shop carefully and until you find quality and comfort—buy the best you can afford—it will help your game because you won't slip, stumble, or blister.

You can use high top tennis shoes. These give excellent ankle support and are heavy and thick soled. For anyone with ankle problems, the high-top is a good idea.

If you have ever had your socks slip in the back every time you hit a shot, you will know that the right kind of socks are important to your feet and game. A good way to solve the slippage problem, and for extra comfort, is to use two pair of socks worn simultaneously. This ensures a tight shoe fit, and a double thickness of socks absorbs more moisture. Thus, you can play longer without feeling like you are stepping in water.

Racquetball shoes and athletic socks

Shorts and Supporters

There is no sense in hindering your game by playing in slacks or pants. Shorts for men and women come in a multitude of styles and colors and look good on men and women (even if you don't have good legs). When you buy your shorts, avoid the bloomer kind that can impede your speed. Look for trim shorts that fit well; the type with slashes at the sides are preferable. This gives you ample leg mobility—never binding and at the same time a snug fit. Gym shorts are good, too: nylon shorts will not absorb perspiration and may cling to the thighs, while cotton will absorb moisture but may cling too much, interfering with movement. Look for nylon blends—there are many. Girls and women generally use tennis-style skirts, and these look fine and probably feel fine, too.

Men can play without supporters, but they do help more than you think. Supporters are sold in small, medium, and large sizes. Buy a good tight-fitting one—a loose one is as worthless as an umbrella in the desert.

Sweatbands and Gloves

Sweatbands wrap around the head and block the sweat from rolling into your eyes from your forehead. Perspiration can be smarting in the eyes. The headband also will keep your hair from obscuring your vision.

A glove worn on the racquet hand helps to keep your hand dry, so when you swing the racquet does not slip. A glove also protects hands from blisters, and if you are just starting to play racquetball, this can be very important. A good solid glove can also have a psychological effect—acting as a touchstone.

An elastic-type grip glove is the best. It has an elastic strip adjustable band around the wrist. The conventional racquetball glove is full-fingered, but there is also a half-finger glove style that also works. Handball gloves are unsatisfactory, because they are thicker and heavier than racquetball gloves and can cause more harm than good because they can interfere with grip. Leather gloves are usually the choice; they stay soft, last longer and are excellent moisture absorbers. The palms are generally made of top-grade deerskin or calfskin. The back of the glove may be nylon or a suitable material. There are also cloth gloves, but these rarely work well.

In place of gloves, some players use a mini-towel tucked into the gym shorts on the right side by the hipbone if you are right-handed, left side if a southpaw. Use of the mini-towel does alleviate some slippage when handling the racquet.

Regulation balls and the full-fingered glove

EYEGUARDS AND SAFETY LENSES

Eyeguards are aluminum tubing or plastic protectors that fit over and shield the eyes. They are cumbersome but do protect the eyes, and if you play a lot they might be considered an essential piece of equipment. Their disadvantage is that they are uncomfortable to wear and obscure peripheral vision, so if you opt for the eyeguard, select one that offers the widest range of vision. Put the eyeshields on and, using your index finger as a focal point, test to see how they allow your sight to extend.

If you already wear glasses, here is one instance where you are fortunate. You can have your glasses purchased in safety lenses (most are now, anyway). Shatterproof lenses afford protection so no supplemental eyeguards are necessary. Contact lenses offer no protection. If you don't wear glasses, you might still want shatterproof lenses instead of eyeguards.

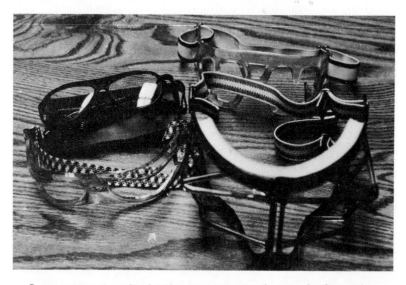

Some eyeguards and safety lenses: protection but maybe discomfort

3

Conditioning

This chapter is an important one, especially if you are over twenty-five years old. It is wise to condition yourself first; do not just rush to the court and start playing because you could cause yourself serious injury. Be sure you are in good physical health, especially you older people. Check with your doctor if you have any minor heart problems or even think you have them. Once you have the okay, start conditioning yourself before running to the courts.

You have to warm up!

THE WARM-UP

You warm up by limbering up before you play. The idea is to stretch these body muscles gradually and get them ready for more strenuous activity. For example, you can stand on your tiptoes twenty times, do a few pushups or situps, and so on. Moderate running or jogging will also start the muscles working to maximum efficiency.

EXERCISES

Here are some simple exercises to get you warmed up for playing:

Toe Reach

Keep feet together and arms out in front; rise up on your toes—hold position for three seconds. Then lower your arms as you return to a normal standing position. Repeat.

Knee Bends

Put hands outstretched in front of you; now assume squatting position; rise up slowly. Repeat.

Sit-ups

Lie on your back with knees bent and feet hooked under a chair rung. Put your hands behind your head and sit up with your right elbow touching your left knee and then repeat with your left elbow touching your right knee. Repeat.

Touch your toes

Keep your feet apart and bend forward to first touch both hands to your left foot, then to your right. Straighten up and repeat.

Pushups

Keep you body and legs straight as you lie on the floor face down. Raise up on your arms and slowly return to floor position. Repeat.

Practice

Simply batting a ball with a tennis racquet against a wall is also good warm up. Fifteen minutes of this conditioning helps immensely to get you ready for the courts. And any old wall will do.

START SLOW

Once you have limbered up or are in fair condition again, do *not* run out and play two hours of racquetball the first day. It is better to start off with a half hour (even if you pay for one hour). Or if you must play the full hour, play moderately without rough competition. Just hit the ball; do not worry just yet about strategy or winning points.

If you play once or twice a week, after a few sessions you can start the more strenuous competitive game. Certainly in a month you will be ready for competition, and indeed should have some then. You can now play confidently because you will not be straining or pulling any muscles. You have warmed up your body. Your muscles will be more flexible, so some straining and stretching will not cause any accidents. In short, take it easy the first few times, gradually increase the pace and then, in a month or so, you will be in good shape.

PHYSICAL PROBLEMS

If you want to play racquetball but have had or still have back problems, first consult with your doctor. Some back problems can be severe; whether you should take racquet in hand at all depends upon your own individual back. Only a doctor can advise you.

If after a while you become exceptionally winded, develop muscle spasms, or encounter other problems, again consult your doctor. Do not keep playing if that leg gives out or the back feels out of whack. It is best to stop and have the problem treated before you do any serious damage.

GENERAL HINTS

If you are going to play sports, almost all experts agree that you should do it regularly after gradually working into it. If you have played racquetball for three months, say, and then stop for three months, do not just plunge back into it. Once again you should condition yourself.

After you play a strenuous hour, do not rush out into cold weather. Instead, relax, take your shower, and change into fresh clothing. Most racquetball courts have suitable locker rooms and shower accommodations.

Part 2

Basics: Grips, Strokes, Serves, and Shots

4

Playing the Game

The racquetball rules are fairly uncomplicated and, after a few times on the court, become rote. Basically, there are only two lines on the court to worry about: the service line and the short line.

Let us look briefly at the game itself and how points are scored.

THE SERVE

To serve, drop the ball to the floor and hit the ball on the *first* bounce. The serve must travel directly to the front wall and rebound to beyond the short line before touching the floor. After the service ball rebounds off the front wall, it can strike a side wall, but it must first bounce beyond the short line before it can hit a third wall.

There are four ways a server can miss the serve and get a second chance:

1. If the served ball hits three walls before touching the floor, a fault is declared; the server is then allowed one more serve.

2. If the served ball does not rebound past the short line, a fault is declared and the server gets another try.

3. If the ball cannons off the front wall to the back wall without first bouncing to the floor, this is a fault. The server tries again.

4. If the ball hits the front wall and then the ceiling, this is a fault.

If a server misses both attempts at a serve—the server thus getting two faults—a side-out results: the opposing player or team serves.

If the served ball does not ever strike the front wall, but instead hits any other surface, this is a side-out; the server loses the serve to the receiver. Thus the server gets no second attempt at a legal serve.

Chapter 6 discusses the serving techniques in detail.

Returning the Serve

To return the serve the opponent (receiver) must stand at least five feet back of the short line; the ball must be returned after it hits the floor past the short line.

The receiver returns the ball to the front wall by using any combination of walls or the ceiling. The receiver must return the serve ball after the first bounce—the ball cannot bounce twice. Also, the receiver's ball must reach the front wall without hitting the floor. Should the ball bounce twice or hit the floor before reaching the front wall, the receiver loses the point to the server.

THE VOLLEY

Once the ball is in play (after the receiver successfully returns it to the wall), the volley ensues. The volley is the alternate hitting of the ball first by the server and then by the receiver. Remember that during a volley the ball may be returned out of mid-air; it does not have to hit the floor. The ball may initially strike any playing surface—side walls, ceiling—but it must always carry to the front wall before bouncing on the floor.

SCORING

Only the server can win points. If the receiver takes the exchange, the receiver gets a side-out rather than a point; in other words, the receiver exchanges position with the server and gets the right to win points.

The goal of racquetball is 21 points; when one of the players reaches that magic number, the game ends. If the game is tied at 20-20, the person who gets the next point wins. There is no overtime or sudden death, as in tennis. Usually, the best two out of three games is the winner. (Beginners might want to play only one game.)

Hinders

There are unforeseen circumstances in any game, and in racquetball they are referred to as hinders. There are two types of hinders: unavoidable and avoidable.

The six unavoidable hinders occur when (1) the ball strikes a light fixture or door handle, (2) the ball hits the opponent after striking the front wall, (3) two players collide, (4) one player makes racquet contact with the other player, (5) the ball carries over the back or side walls after the front wall return, or (6) a ball hits the front wall on the serve and on the rebound goes into the gallery. The play goes (starts) over. Also, one player's body blocking the other player's view of the ball—such as when a ball passes between the legs of one player—results in what is called a screen shot. This, too, is a play over.

The three avoidable hinders occur when (1) one player does not move to allow the opponent to return the ball, (2) the player deliberately blocks the opponent's return shot to the front wall, or (3) one player deliberately pushes or shoves during a hit volley. If the ball goes out of the court, such as careening off a racquet edge, before it is returned to the front wall, this is a side-out or point against the player who hit it out.

THE GRIP: FOREHAND AND BACKHAND STROKES

The grip—how you hold your racquet—determines how well you deliver the foreward and back strokes of the game, your forehand and backhand strokes. If you have a good solid grip on the racquet, you will get the required power and control; an incorrect grip obviously will not deliver the ball properly.

Forehand Stroke

This stroke is the meat-and-potatoes of good playing, so learn it well. It saves a great deal of complicated strategy if you can wear your opponent down with good forehand strokes.

The forehand grip is basically a handshake clasp with a trigger

Fig. 4-1. The forehand grip

finger (see figure 4-1). Pick up the racquet at the throat area and hold it in front of your body at navel height. Keep the string face of the racquet perpendicular to the floor (see figures 4-2, 4-3). Be sure that the handle is properly set in your hand. Think or visualize a straight line drawn along the top surface of the racquet handle. This imaginary line from the throat of the racquet to your hand should exactly intersect the "V" formed by your thumb and index finger grasping the handle. Look down at your hand on the racquet—that is where the "V" should be. With this grip you will get maximum power and accuracy.

If the grip is not exactly as just stated—remember the V—the racquet will be twisted in your hand. This results in bad shots. For example, if the top of the racquet is slanted backward, you will slice the ball. If the top face of the racquet is slanted forward, you will most probably hit the ball into the floor. For further accuracy, extend your index figure about 1/2 inch toward the racquet throat. This is known as the trigger finger grip and gives you more control of the shot.

Fig. 4-2. Racquet head perpendicular to floor

Fig. 4-3. Step into the ball

The butt of the racquet should rest in the heel of your hand; it should be against the fleshy part of your palm. If you hold the handle too high, your stroke will be faulted. Similarly, holding the handle in a low grip can cause you to lose the racquet completely on a hard-hit ball.

To execute the forehand stroke, face the right side wall if you are right-handed, the left wall if you are left-handed. Keep your feet apart about shoulder-width and your knees slightly bent. Grasp your racquet with the proper forehand grip and swing (see figure 4-4).

Fig. 4-4. The forehand stroke

Figs. 4-4 cont.

An example of the forehand cross-court drive is shown in figure 4-5.

1. Swing your racquet from a starting backswing position, follow through, then swing back to the backswing, and so on. The stroke should be smooth and rhythmical, never static or jerky if you want the ball to go where desired.

2. The backswing is when the racquet is behind the head, your wrist is fully cocked. Bend your elbow about 90 degrees and keep the racquet near your ear. Then swing and follow through.

3. To get some power in the stroke, step into the swing. Step forward, with your left toe pointed in the direction of the right front corner of the court (have your right toes pointed to the left front corner if you are left-handed). The front foot should lead the shot to where you are aiming the ball. Your front foot should be pointed forward at about the same time the racquet swings past your left ankle.

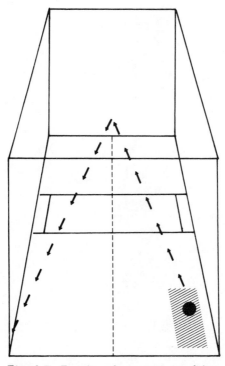

Fig. 4-5. Forehand cross-court drive

The Backhand Stroke

The backhand stroke seems like an awkward shot; actually, it is one of the most graceful strokes if done properly. Some players use the forehand grip as their backhand stroke, but it is much better to use the real backhand. This grip is similar to the forehand except that the handle is rotated within your hand about one-eighth of a full turn, with the top of the racquet tilting toward, not away from, the wall. Here is how to execute the backhand stroke (see figures 4-6, 4-7):

Figs. 4-6, 4-7. The Backhand Stroke   (shown on page 36)
Figs. 4-8, 4-9. The Follow Through

1. Position your body with your feet *almost* parallel to the front wall; your left side (or right side if you are left handed) should be pointed toward the front wall.

2. Face the left (or right) side of the wall when you are ready to swing. Thus, your left or right side will be pointed at the front wall and your feet will be almost parallel to the same wall.

3. Bring the racquet into a backswing or cocked position near your left (or right) ear. For the downswing, put your body

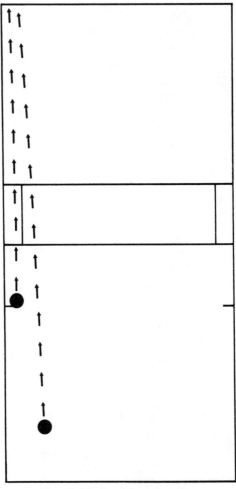

Fig. 4-10. Backhand volley

weight mostly on your left (or right) foot, thus slightly twisting your lower torso. Your hips will rotate around to the left (or right), and your right (or left) shoulder will be tucked in somewhat.

4. As you sweep the racquet downward, uncoil your hips and transfer your weight to the front foot (see figures 4-8, 4-9). Straighten your arm as the racquet leads with the foot so the racquet handle passes nearly parallel to the floor. Do not dip or slant the handle.

5. The follow through is low and smooth. Snap the wrist somewhat to give power to the stroke. The wrist snap occurs when you contact with the ball. As in the foreward stroke, the step forward ensures anterior body momentum: the hips uncoil from the rear to the front foot.

An example of strategic backhand volley placement is shown in figure 4-10.

If you learn these two basic strokes first and learn them well, you are on your way. More elaborate strokes and defensive plays are coming up.

5

Common Do's and Don'ts on Basic Strokes

In time, with practice, you can master most racquetball shots. No matter whether beginner or advanced player, however, there are do's and don'ts associated with basic sound technique.

FOREHAND GRIP

The way you grip your racquet does make a difference. Generally if your grip is poor—the hand slips to the right or left—the ball will hit the floor short of the wall. Hold the racquet so your thumb and forefinger make a "V" along the handle when the racquet face is perpendicular to the floor. Maintain a tight grip on the racquet just before and during the moment of impact.

BACKHAND GRIP

If you are using the forehand grip to make a backhand shot (and some players do), you might rotate the head of the racquet upward. This causes the ball to hit up high on the wall making an easy return for your opponent. It is far better to move the gripping hand a quarter- to half-inch on the shaft for the backhand stroke. This stroke keeps the face of the racquet perpendicular to the floor when you hit the ball. This will give you the accuracy to hit the ball where you want it because the tilt of the racquet makes up for the difference in wrist position between forehand and backhand stroke.

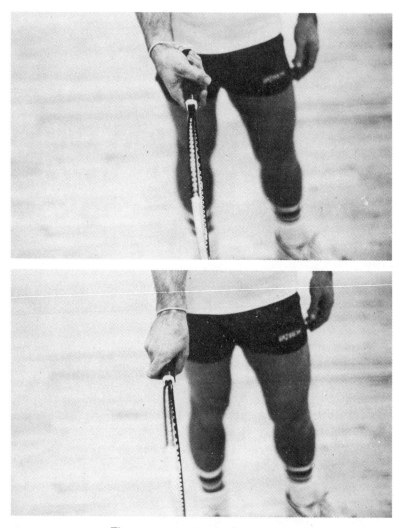

The wrong way to grip the racquet

SERVING

Hitting the ball when it is too close to your body—your elbow against your body—results in a weak shot, generally hitting the wall too high and making an easy return for your opponent. Always drop the ball away from and in front of the body when serving. This will give you space and time for a full swing. A good hard serve is a ball that is dropped below knee level and hit at this position so you get a low, hard drive path to the wall.

FOREHAND SWING

When you are getting ready to hit the ball assume the proper position.

- Don't keep knees too straight or stiff.
- Don't hold the racquet below the waist.
- Don't be flatfooted; be ready to move.

The incorrect grip and balance

BACKSWING

The proper backswing to your forehand or backhand shot allows you to hit the ball accurately and to get off a good offensive shot.

Do not start the backswing too late—be ready. Pivot your body and hips sideways so you have better balance and leverage.

- Don't keep wrist stiff. Be sure to cock your wrist.
- Don't keep weight on both feet. Keep your weight on the back foot.
- Don't keep feet too far apart; feet should be shoulder-width apart—never more.
- Don't keep elbow near the body; keep your arm away from your side and never rigidly bent.
- Don't make the backswing too low. This causes loss of racquet speed and power.

Faulty backswing

CONTACT POINT

In the forehand stroke your elbow should lead as you start the downward arc and you want to hit the ball a few inches above your instep or before the ball reaches the front foot. At this contact point the wrist is snapped forward so there is solid contact of racquet on ball.

The ball is either hit out of the air, after it bounces and starts the upward swing, or after the bounce and near the end of the downward arc. Try to strike the ball at ankle level after it bounces and is in the downward arc.

- Don't cramp your swing and hit the ball too close to the body.
- Don't lift your head and lose sight of the ball.
- Don't keep your knees too stiff as you hit the ball.

Contact point too far in front

Follow through should not be a lunge like this one

- Don't angle your racquet, keep it parallel to the floor.
- Don't swing at the ball with your arms only, use the motion of your entire body.

FOLLOW THROUGH

Many players think that if they hit the ball squarely and low, that is all there is to it. Wrong. You must make the follow through swing so the ball hits the wall with power and accuracy. Your racquet arm must swing naturally across your body after you hit the ball.

- Don't make a half stroke—you will hit a weak shot.
- Don't tense up; when you hear the ball strike the racquet keep the arm moving.
- Do not stand in the same place after the ball is struck; move quickly to the best court position.

The Serve and Return of Serve

Because the server is the only player who can score a point, it is imperative that you learn to serve accurately and properly. A good serve can win or lose a game, and serving—a really excellent serve—gives you a distinct advantage right away.

The service boundaries on the court are the two parallel red lines, about five feet apart, that run from side wall to side wall. Standing in a center-court position will give you more leeway for initiating an attack of various serves rather than standing to one side or another when serving. It also forces your opponent to stand in the center of the court.

KINDS OF SERVES

Your serve can be driving, lob, a Z ball, or even a garbage serve. The secret to the successful serve is not so much the type of serve (although that does matter) as keeping your opponent off guard. The idea of any type of serve is to force your opponent to make a quick return, and any quick return without thought may be a bad one. When the return of the serve is poor, you have a good chance to capture the point.

Drive Serve

The drive serve is a very fast, low, and hot ball aimed at the back court corners. Your opponent must move in a hurry to get the serve and thus may not be able to return the ball properly.

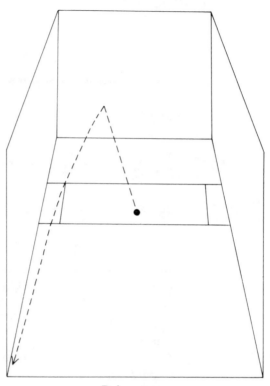

Drive serve

The drive serve should strike the front wall only a few feet right or left of center.

To make a drive serve, stand in the center of the service area; drop the ball and take a short step forward and make contact. The ball must rebound off the front wall low and fast and travel back into the back court in the direction of either far corner. Hit the serve a few feet to the left (or right) of the center of the front wall so it rebounds into the deep left (or right) corner, making a return almost impossible.

Remember that as you move your target closer to the side wall, the rebound may hit the side wall, causing the ball to go out into center court and thus making it easier for your opponent to get at it. In other words, your opponent will not have to get to the ball—it will go to your opponent. So keep the drive serve off the side wall. It is also important to remember that even though the drive serve should be hit hard, it should not be struck so hard that it rebounds off the back wall. The good drive serve should bounce just after it passes the short line and, if not hit as a return, bounce again just before it reaches the back wall.

A fast and low drive serve will usually result in a hard hit return from your opponent. Thus, after you serve, step back a few feet.

Lob Serve

The lob serve, whether medium or high, makes for a difficult return.

The medium lob serve should strike the front wall about eight feet from the floor so it bounces three to four feet past the short line. This serve is most effective when the ball is hit near the side wall. And, as in the drive serve, the medium lob serve should not strike the side wall or the ball will rebound into center court, giving your opponent an easy shot.

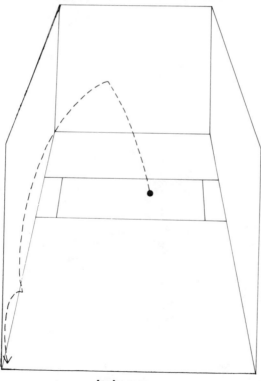

Lob serve

The high lob serve is hit so it strikes the front wall a few feet higher than the low lob. Thus the high lob has a higher bounce. The high lob should bounce and arc toward the corner, staying near the side of the wall.

To serve the lob, stand inside the server's area, as for the drive serve. Drop the ball—keep your body upright—and strike the ball when it reaches your waist height. Do *not* snap your wrist as you do with other strokes; keep your wrist stiff, to prevent the ball from going into the back wall after it bounces. The ball will float after it strikes the front wall—the ball's speed will be reduced. The idea is to have the serve bounce a few feet past the short line so it reaches your opponent at chest level. In such a position your opponent is hard put to connect with a good solid hit.

The *garbage serve* is a half-lob serve where the ball carries just beyond the short line and bounces in a high arc so it dies at the back wall—a frustrating serve to return if done properly.

Lob serve

Lob serve

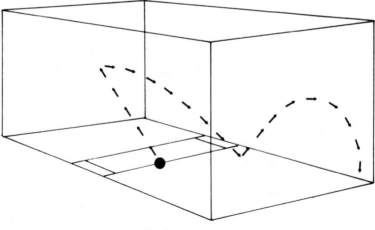

Garbage serve

Z Serve

The Z serve is hit so that it strikes the front wall as close to the side wall as possible and then careens off the side wall, crosses the court in the air, and bounces just before it reaches the opposite side wall. The change of direction of the Z serve is what keeps your opponent off balance. This ball generally rebounds toward the mid-court area, putting the ball in a very difficult spot for a good return.

The serving position for the Z ball is the same as for other serves. The ball must be hit quickly and sharply into the front wall just before it strikes the side wall. The motion is like the drive serve, except that at the last moment the server should be able to strike the ball into either front wall corner. Remember in the Z serve that the ball must hit the front wall first, or you lose the serve. If the Z serve does not bounce before it reaches the opposite side wall, a fault results.

If you strike the ball low and hard to the front wall, the ball will rebound off the opposite side wall low and hard, possibly resulting in a drive return. Be prepared for this. If the serve is struck high on the front wall, the ball generally will rebound off the opposite side wall at chest level.

The Z serve

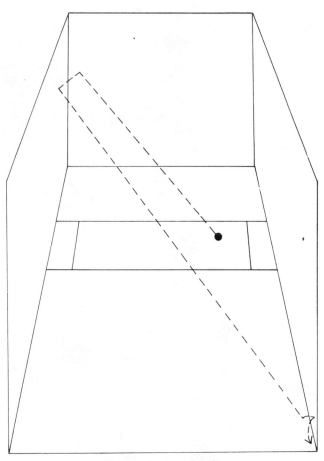

Z-serve flight of ball

BASIC RETURNS

If the server can force a weak return, the odds of the server winning the point are favorable. Thus it is imperative that you know how to return a serve. The three basic returns of serves are (1) strong-side pass shot, (2) cross-court pass shot, and (3) ceiling ball return.

The strong-side pass shot is good to use against a drive or lob serve. This shot is hit hard so the ball rebounds off the front wall and stays near the side wall but does not strike it as it travels into the back court. This is an effective shot because the server must move quickly from midcourt over to the side wall to cut it off—this is not easy.

The cross-court pass shot is a good general return that should strike the front wall in the center and rebound to the opposite court. The cross-court pass shot should not hit the side wall until it passes the server. If it does, the ball will rebound into the center court, where it can be reached easily by your opponent.

The ceiling ball return is effective against any serve, but it is difficult to execute for most players because the backhand motion from either the waist or chest is difficult to time.

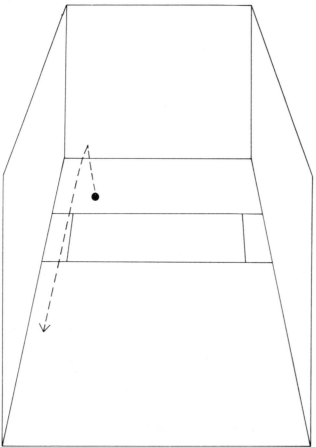

Pass shot

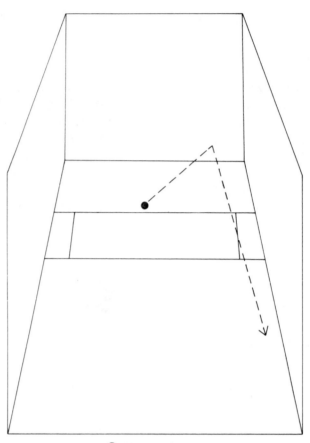

Cross-court pass

The Z ball return is an effective—but risky—shot, one that the beginner would be better off learning at a more advanced stage in his or her career.

To return any serve, stand a few feet from the back wall in the middle of the court; you have enough space to move to either side wall once the serve is hit. Stand with your waist and knees slightly bent and your body weight evenly distributed. In this position you can move quickly either right or left.

If the serve is hit to the left (or right) corner, pivot on your left (or right) foot, using your right (or left) foot as the lead step. If the serve is hit to the right (or left) corner, then pivot on your right (or left) foot, with your left (or right) foot making the lead step.

SERVICE HINTS

Your serves can mean points for you; don't consider it just a shot hit against the wall for your opponent to return.

1. Take your time and think before you hit the ball—put it where your opponent ain't. Later on, you will learn that serving right at your opponent—at certain strategic times—may be an effective way to keep your opponent off-balance. However, for now, go for the part of the court that would be most difficult for your opponent to reach.

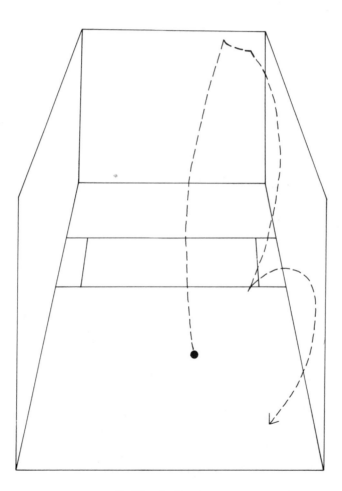

Ceiling ball return

2. Never hit the back wall. If you slam a serve and it comes off the back wall, your opponent can kill the ball and win the point.

3. Serve deeply so you'll have time to get into center-court defensive position. (The importance of center-court position is discussed in chapter 11.)

4. Drop the ball away from and in front of the body so you will have enough space for a full swing.

5. Avoid the middle of the court when serving; keep your opponent guessing by alternating serves into corners.

6. "Psych" out your opponent; study him just before you serve so he will know you know where he is.

7

Four Vital Defensive Shots

As in most games, there are certain vital or defensive moves or strokes you must know to play racquetball effectively. In racquetball these are the *ceiling ball,* the *around-the-wall-ball,* the *Z ball,* and the *lob.* To play the game skillfully you should learn these basic shots, whether for defense, returns, or whatever. How you use them depends on your opponent and the run of the game.

THE CEILING BALL

The ceiling ball is the most effective defensive shot in racquetball and can be played from almost any position on the court, with either a forehand or backhand. The purpose of the ceiling ball is to move your opponent out of the midcourt area into the back court area. If executed properly, the ball bounces high toward the back wall, arcing as it does so.

The ceiling ball is not easy to hit; it requires time and practice, but it is the strongest defensive shot you can play. The ceiling shot is played directly up to the ceiling, near the juncture of the ceiling with the front wall. The ceiling target is one to five feet from the front wall. If you fail to strike within this area, the ball will come up short—hit midcourt—and open the door for a kill by your opponent. The ball hitting the side takes away the deep-court effectiveness: it puts the ceiling ball in the middle of the court without the arc effect. The ceiling shot is

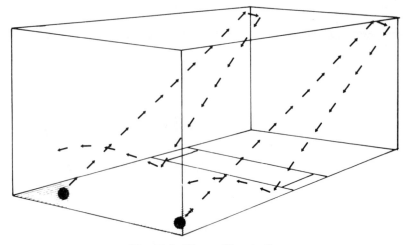

Fig. 7-1. The ceiling ball

done with a hard hit directed toward your opponent's backhand side.

The best ceiling shot first strikes the ceiling, then the front wall, and then zooms to the floor, rebounding high. The rebound should be very near the back wall, thus making it almost impossible for the opponent to return it (see figure 7-1).

The two types of ceiling shots most often used are the forehand overhead ceiling return and the backhand overhead (waist-high) ceiling stroke. The waist-high ceiling stroke is used for hitting low balls. Involving an underhand flip of the wrist, this shot will give you a chance to recover court position if you are in a bad court spot and off balance.

Forehand Overhead Ceiling Shot

Execute the forehand ceiling shot with an overhand stroke. Try to have your racquet hit the ball head high and about a foot ahead of your head, off the front toe. (In a moment we tell you. how to practice.) The rear-to-front foot weight and follow through will ensure the power necessary to get the ball where you want it, not where your opponent wants it.

Fig. 7-2. Forehand overhead ceiling shot

To start the swing, keep the knees slightly bent and the racquet in position near the left ear. Rotate your hips to the left (or to the right if you are left-handed), and swerve the right (or left) shoulder down into a tucked position. As you move your hips and shoulders, your body weight will shift to your back left (or right) foot.

You are now ready to uncoil and strike the ball with a thrusting forward motion. Twist your hips around to the right (or left) (toward the front wall), and move your right (or left) shoulder out of the tuck position and stroke the ball.

Keep your racquet hand stiff and extended as you get ready to strike the ball; upon contact your wrist will snap slightly, imparting an undercut action that creates ball speed. Hit the ball waist high or slightly higher, depending on where the ball presents itself. Keep the racquet slanted backward (open-faced) so you can get the upward angle.

To practice the forehand overhead ceiling shot, face the side wall and use the forehand position. Toss the ball above your head, as you would if you were making a tennis serve. Strike the ball after it has peaked and started its descent to the floor. To swing, extend your racquet arm from the forehand position to near your ear and then to the ball. Try to strike the ball so it hits the ceiling as close to the front wall as possible. Make the contact point occur just in front of your body, above your head and over your lead foot. Then follow through with the racquet pointing to the floor.

Always point your lead foot backward, pointing to the front wall, with your back foot turned and pointing to the side wall. This gives you the push you need to reach up and swing with power. Make contact with the ball in front of your body over your lead foot, and move into position quickly.

The Backhand Overhead Ceiling Return

The backhand overhead ceiling ball is an effective return of your opponent's ceiling ball. This is a difficult shot, requiring a backhand swing over your head from deep-court position.

The same principles that apply to the regular backhand stroke are in effect for this shot. Get into the standard backhand position and drop the ball, as you do when practicing a standard stroke. Hold the racquet across your body until your lead foot steps into the swing. As you move your arm forward, drop your nonracquet shoulder slightly—this elevates the racquet shoulder and opens the face of the racquet when it makes contact with the ball. The open face (strings tilted slightly to the ceiling) makes hitting the ball upward easier.

As you swing, snap your wrist just before you make contact with the ball. Again, strike the ball out in front of your body and over your lead foot. The lower the ball drops to the floor, the more effort is necessary to hit the ball upward toward the ceiling. Follow through with the standard backhand stroke, with your racquet just a little higher upon contact and completion.

Practice the backhand overhead ceiling shot by letting the ball bounce first. But instead of catching the ball after the bounce, move into position and, using an overhead stroke, strike the ball back to the ceiling. To do this, position your racquet in the standard backhand position until you want to step to contact the ball. Then raise your racquet and drive your elbow forward. The wrist should snap naturally just before you make contact with the ball; the follow through leaves your racquet arm bent, with your racquet above your head. Avoid making contact with the ball too close to the body because this causes you to hit the ball with an uneven racquet face, and the ball will probably slice off into a side wall. The most effective contact is made slightly out in front of the body.

AROUND-THE-WALL BALL

The around-the-wall ball is not a difficult shot and can be mastered after only a little playing. The ball is generally struck waist high from deep court (three-quarter court), usually with a backhand shot (see figure 7-3). The ball is sent cross court with moderate drive, striking the side walls high in the front right (or left) corner. The point of contact with the ball should coincide with your right (or left) foot forward. Start with a normal backhand position, and then arc around like a baseball player swinging a bat left-handed (or right-handed). Aim the ball so it hits

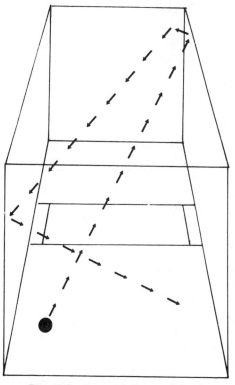

Fig. 7-3. Around-the-wall ball

first on the side wall, about three feet down from the ceiling and three feet in from the front wall. Even if you miss the 3-foot preferred spot—a couple of feet either way—the ball will still do its trick. The ball should *not* strike the ceiling at all.

The ball will wrap around the corner in a diagonal direction toward the left (or right) side wall and hit at midcourt (about two-thirds of the way up) and then angle down to the floor.

There is a forehand around-the-wall ball, but it is not recommended because it usually comes off the right (or left) side wall right into your opponent's powerful forehand.

THE Z BALL

The *Z* shot is so called because it makes the letter *Z* during its course of flight. Execute the shot by using any stroke (forehand, backhand, overhead) to about eight feet or higher on the front wall so that the ball hits sharp and fast and immediately

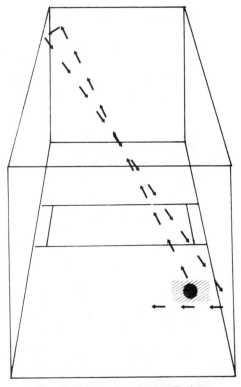

Fig. 7-4. The forehand Z shot

rebounds to the side wall, from where it crosses court through the air and rebounds off the opposite wall. As the ball makes its path, it picks up speed and spin and so it is difficult to return.

During a rally, hit the Z ball to the front wall, side wall, and opposite wall—all on the fly. In this way your opponent is forced out of the front court to the back court area in chase of a return. Because the return is difficult, this shot should result in an easy setup point for you. In essence, the effective Z ball forces your opponent into a bad court position and a weak or nonreturnable action.

The most satisfactory Z ball is a forehand shot hit as near the front wall and as close to the right side wall as possible. Hit the forehand Z ball by standing just behind the second short line and about three feet from the right (or left) side wall. Hit the ball waist high with moderate power so it carries well. Your

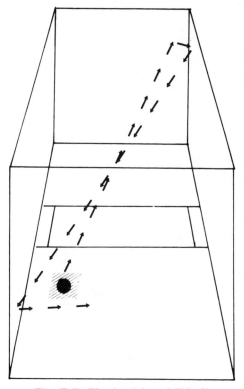

Fig. 7-5. The backhand Z ball

target for the ball is a spot three feet down from the ceiling and three feet in from the left (or right) side wall. Drive the ball hard and cross court so it strikes the front wall first. If you do not hit the forehand *Z* ball properly, the ball will end up somewhere midcourt or off the backwall, giving your opponent the advantage.

The forehand *Z* ball strikes the front wall high at the left (or right) corner, cuts quickly into the left (or right) side wall, and then trajects diagonally cross-court to the right (or left) side wall, rebounding at an angle almost parallel to the back wall, about a foot or so out (see figures 7-4, 7-5).

An overhead or knee-high Z ball should be hit high enough so it can go across court once it has hit the front and side walls—usually at a height of about eight feet. To get the spin necessary to make any Z ball effective, hit it hard, with the point of contact on the front wall within a foot or so of the side wall.

Practice the *Z* ball to become accustomed to the angles and changes of direction the ball will take. To practice, position yourself in the midcourt area. Hit the ball with an overhead stroke into the front wall near either side wall. Try to locate just the right spot for the *Z* ball to hit—once you have the target you can vary your shots by moving around the floor and changing how hard you hit the ball. This practice will give you an idea of how hard you have to strike the ball in relation to the portion of the court you are standing. It will also show you the weak points of hitting a poor *Z* ball as you watch its return position on the court.

LOB

A lob return is not easy to do but a well placed lob can catch your opponent flatfooted. Hit the lob shot firmly with a high arcing stroke; you want the ball to hit the front wall near the ceiling. A good lob rebounds to hit the floor behind the short line and bounces high, coming down again close to the back wall but not touching it.

8

Beginner's Pitfalls

No matter what your sport is—racquetball, tennis, or hand-ball—there are certain pitfalls that beginners should be aware of at the start. These are the little things that can make the difference between becoming an adequate player or a superlative one. Failing to take aggressive advantage of a position or not completing a swing, for example, are actually pitfalls that affect your game.

SERVING READINESS

Always be ready when serving—before you serve, glance at your opponent so you know exactly where he is and so he knows you know. Notice whether he or she is leaning to one side or the other.

EARLY STROKE

Here is a common pitfall: Striking the ball before it is in proper position will result in less power on the ball and an easy return for your opponent. Don't make your stroke until the ball passes the center of your body. Hold off until the ball is exactly in this position. Then, when you hit the ball, it will have good speed and hit the wall much lower, making a return difficult.

STIFF-WRIST STROKE

The wrist should be stiff when hitting the ball, but it should never be rigid. A rigid wrist pushes the ball to the wall rather than stroking it to the wall—there is less power. Hold your wrist cocked well back at the start of the stroke, and when you hit the ball snap or roll over the wrist action slightly. This will give power to the ball and result in a difficult shot for your opponent to return.

BACKHAND FLOP

If you don't take a full backhand swing, you will swat the ball instead of hitting it. If your thumb position shifts, the ball will go toward the ceiling. Poor body position generally causes the flop. Again, be sure the face of the racquet is perpendicular to the floor.

ELBOW SHOT

Holding your elbow crimped with arm against the body will result in the shot having little power and direction. Be sure your arm is extended in a swing arc.

OVERHAND OVERUSE

When a ball comes from the deep court off the wall and bounces high off the back wall, there is the natural temptation to return it with an overhand stroke. Wait until you can get in position for the sidearm stroke (forehand or backhand). You will be able to control the ball much easier.

CAT IN A CORNER

Put yourself in a corner and you will indeed be cornered. You will be too close to the back wall to make any kind of effective swing. Always know how much space you have relative to the walls and especially corners.

BACK WALL REBOUNDS

Do not rush to hit a ball before it can rebound off the back wall. If your body is parallel to the front and back walls you can only hit a weak shot. Time the ball so you can swing your body into proper hitting position as the ball comes off the wall. Never let the ball crowd your shot. Leave enough room to take a full swing.

AGAINST THE WALL CONTORTIONS

In certain deep-court situations the back wall can be a stumbling block that makes a beginning player resort to ice skating contortions. Hit the rear wall shot as you would a front wall shot. Time your stroke and don't end up being a whirling dervish and losing a point.

CEILING SHOT

If you try a ceiling shot when you are close in, you will make an easy set-up point for your opponent. Make the ceiling shot from deep court.

OVERSWINGING

This is a common error and tough to resist. Hitting the ball harder than really necessary can result in more harm than good. Try to strike the ball with just enough force to keep your opponent back and making defensive shots. Overswinging is a plague and only practice can eliminate it.

BACKHAND CEILING SHOT

Most players' backhand shots are weaker than their forehand strokes and less accurate. Chances are good that by pressing your shoulder to the wall you can hit an overhand ceiling shot with your forehand and have more control and power. Of course, if the ball is a real wallpaper hanger, you will have to resort to the backhand stroke.

OVERCONFIDENCE

When many players make a kill shot or a perfect return, they assume there will be no return from the opponent and thus, stand still. Not so. After hitting the ball—move! Even if you think you have a winner, get moving and head for that center-court position. Never stay in the same spot you made your hit from—the percentages are against you.

KILL SHOT

A kill try too close to your opponent generally just does not work. You must always allow that your kill shot may not be perfect. Use the kill shot when you are away from your opponent. Then the speed and bounce off the side wall to front wall will work to your advantage. Hitting away from your opponent rather than to him gives you the percentage.

DOUBLE TROUBLE

In doubles, there is always confusion as to who hits what and the result might be two racquets banging in unison in thin air. The player on the forehand side should take the shot that comes down the middle between the two partners. See chapter 12 on doubles play.

FOREHAND CEILING STROKE

The general stroke of the ceiling ball is basically the same as the forehand stroke, but there are a few differences. On the backswing bring the racquet back to a position behind your head. When you are ready to hit the ball, keep your racquet directly behind your back—your elbows should be pointing to the ceiling. Make the forward swing with an upward motion and extend your entire body toward the ceiling. Remember that the higher the point of contact with the ball, the better the chances are of the ball having zip behind it. End the stroke with a step forward to help maintain balance.

- Don't keep your weight on the back foot—weight should be on front foot when ball is hit.

- Don't stop the racquet behind the head; keep it moving backward.

- Don't let the ball drop so low that it is difficult to hit it with a full stroke.

- Don't, after hitting the ball, stay anchored to the spot; put foot forward to maintain good balance and prepare for next shot.

SERVING

When you go to the service box, take your time. This is your advantage shot; use it well. Don't stand too close to either side wall; this limits the choice of service direction. When serving the bread-and-butter drive serve:

● Don't make contact with the ball too high; you will be at a disadvantage and the strike will be bad.

● Don't sacrifice control for speed; best to hit only as hard as accuracy will allow.

● Don't hit the ball so hard that it strikes high off the wall and rebounds off the back wall for an easy set up.

● Don't make the angle of service too acute; this could result in the ball rebounding off the side wall into center court for an easy set up.

● Don't use the same serve each time—your opponent will begin to expect what is coming.

OBSERVATION

This is last but definitely not the least in the pitfall parlay. To make that perfect shot you should always know the location of your opponent. For example, let's say you just hit the ball to your opponent who is behind you. If you don't turn your head to see what he is doing, he will put the ball past you. So again, keep your eye on your opponent *and the ball.* It is tough to do both, but try. After you hit a ball, observe the ball on its way to your opponent. Try not to change your body position but rather use a neck-swiveling motion. Keep your head moving and eyes alert. After some play, this action will come automatically.

Part 3

Strategy: Order in the Court!

9

Offensive Strategy

For good offensive play, you will need an array of different shots and three good ones are the pass shot, the kill shot, and the drop shot. Each is played differently; none are difficult to master.

THE PASS SHOT

The pass shot is as essential to your play as the racquet. It is a shot aimed to pass your opponent rather than a ball your opponent can easily return. This is a bread-and-butter shot and part of all good play. It can be played down the line (backhand) or cross-court, either backhand or forehand.

Down-the-Line Pass

The down-the-line pass is almost always executed on the left (or right) or backhand side of the court, with the player fairly deep in this court position. The standard backhand stroke is used. Hit the ball anywhere from your knee to navel height; the ball should strike the front wall one to three feet from the left (or right) side wall (see figures 9-1, 9-2). The idea is to get the ball to rebound off the front wall rather low, about three feet up from the floor, and skim back along the same side wall to the back court. The difficult part of the shot is keeping the ball close to the wall, that is, parallel to it. If the ball strikes the side wall, it ricochets usually into midcourt—not an enviable

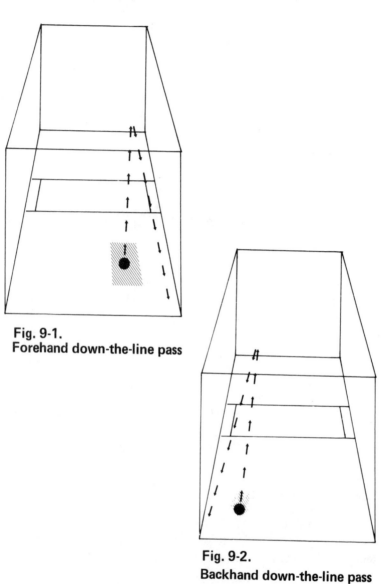

Fig. 9-1.
Forehand down-the-line pass

Fig. 9-2.
Backhand down-the-line pass

place for you because then your opponent can do anything with it. If you can, put a spin on the ball so it is less likely to strike the side wall. This is done with a quick slicing stroke hitting the lower half of the ball in a vertical motion. It is not easy and takes practice.

Cross-Court Pass

The cross-court ball, termed the V-ball (the flight path makes a letter "V") can be executed forehand or backhand. For two right-handed players the more effective shot is the forehand cross-court because it is hit to the opponent's backhand. And since it is a forehand stroke, you can get more power into it.

Although the cross-court pass can be done close to the front

The pass shot stroke

wall, it is usually hit from a more distant position on the court. Make contact with the ball at knee to waist height. Take a step or two back, and make a smooth stroke at the ball. The ball should strike the wall two to four feet high and then be propelled to the backhand rear court. There it is generally difficult for the opponent to play.

The secret of the cross-court pass is how wide and how high the ball is hit. It should be wide enough to hit the center of the front wall, although a foot to the left (or right) will make the ball travel at a wider angle—all the better. The ball will then have more chance of carrying past your opponent's outstretched racquet. If the ball is too far to the right (or left)—two feet, say—the ball will travel directly to your opponent's racquet.

Striking the ball at right height is also important. The ball should strike the wall two to four feet high for the most effect. However, a ball gains elevation after striking the racquet and so usually hits higher. Aim for one to three feet above the wall and let the ball (or gravity) do the rest.

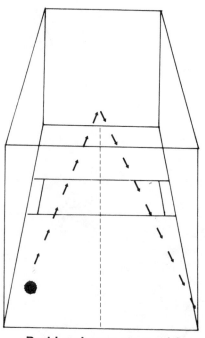

Backhand cross-ccourt drive

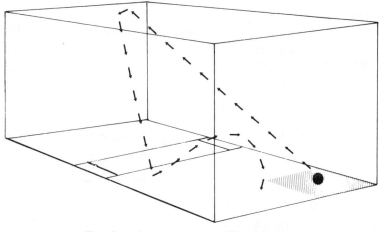

Forehand cross-court ceiling shot

Cross-Court Ceiling Shot

The cross-court ceiling shot is hit from a position right or left of the center court and aims for the center of the ceiling. The ball strikes the ceiling and then the front wall and veers toward the corner opposite you.

How hard should you hit the ball for these passes? Generally, with about 70 percent power, although beginners should practice with less power until they have some expertise with the shot.

STRATEGY FOR PASS SHOTS

The successful pass shot is a ball that is hit away from your opponent. It should hit past your opponent without rebounding high enough off the back wall to be played. It should also be hit without rebounding off the back wall to the side walls because if the ball does hit the side wall, it rebounds back into the center court area, making it easy to return.

Practice pass shots with a friend; your friend should stand in the server's area and serve all different ways to you. Control is the key to success in the pass shot; it is not as important to hit low shots as it is to strike the shot exactly *when* you want it so it goes where you want it.

THE KILL SHOT

The kill shot is a ball that hits so low on the front wall and with such force that it is unreturnable. This is a vital racquetball shot and can win you many points, and it is not that difficult to master. You hit the kill shot with either the forehand or the backhand stroke.

If you hit the ball too low for the kill shot, it will bounce or skip before it hits the front wall losing the point, so accuracy is vital. If you hit the ball too high, it will come off the front wall so your opponent can return it easily.

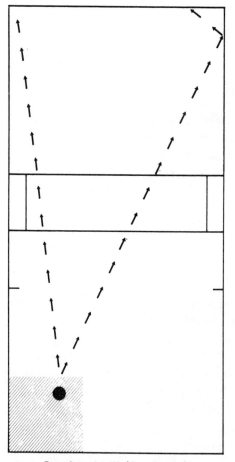

Overhead kill (forehand)

The kill shot may be a side-wall front-wall hit or a ball that strikes the front-wall side-wall or a ball that is hit off the back wall. It also may be a straight side-wall front-wall shot—this is the most common. This latter shot can be mastered in short time while the others take some doing.

To make the straight kill shot, hit the ball low when it is about a foot off the ground. You will have to bend your body and your knees to do it.

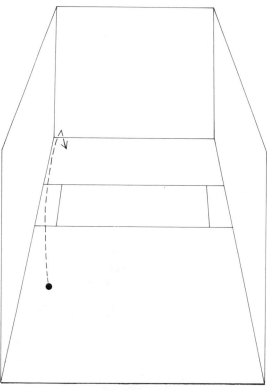

Straight kill

Hitting the kill to the front wall first is done usually by hitting the ball cross-court away from your opponent hoping that the ball bounces low on the side wall and dies.

If you are hitting the kill shot off the back wall, wait for the ball to come to you and then hit it as you would a normal straight kill shot directly to the front wall.

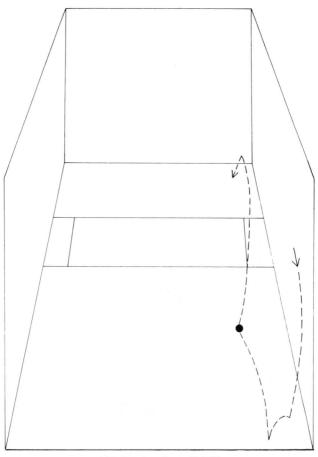

Off-the-back-wall kill

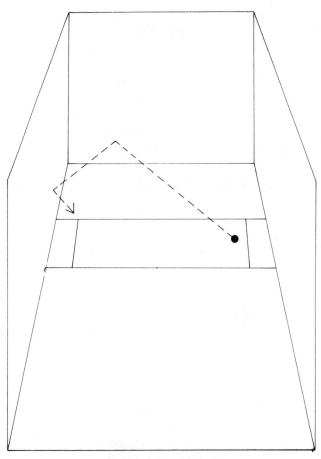

Front-side-wall kill

THE DROP SHOT

The drop shot is not a hard-hit shot but it can win points if done properly. When you are near the front wall and your opponent is near the back wall, move up rapidly and hit the ball softly at an angle toward the front wall. With luck the ball will drop against the front wall and almost die before your opponent can scurry to it.

Also, the surprise of the drop shot makes it a good candidate for a winner. It is a deliberate slow ball mixup to catch your opponent off-guard and as such must be controlled. Do not swing too much—rather just catch the ball on your racquet and push it gently toward the front wall. What you don't want to do is hit the ball hard so that it comes off the front wall with any zing because then your opponent will be able to catch up to it and make a return.

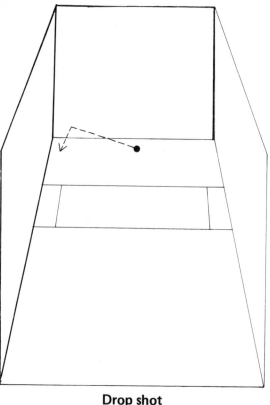

Drop shot

10

Playing
the Back Wall

No matter how you play racquetball, returning off the back
wall is an important part of the game, which is what this chapter is all about. Back wall play depends upon keeping your eye
on the ball (you always should, anyway) and excellent footwork and balance. You must be in the right place and hit at the
right time. How much time you have to get to the ball dictates
just how fast you must react to hit the ball.

You can probably return a backhand shot without too much
problem, but the kind of return is important. You can kill the
ball, drive it, use the ceiling ball, or a variety of shots. Let us
look at the set up for the backhand wall shot

FOOTWORK

The minute you see the ball carrying from the front wall
toward the back wall, turn and start in the same direction as the
ball. When the ball strikes the back wall, follow it again and
turn toward the front wall. This fancy footwork requires fluid
body movement and muscle coordination as you watch the ball
make its flight. Then you can apply the forehand or backhand
return.

Exercises

To get the feet moving and to achieve proper coordination,
practice a bit. Find a wall—any wall—and face it from three feet

back. Now turn sideways, face an imaginary right (or left) side wall, get in the forehand position, and retreat back with a sideway shuffle. Then stop within five feet of an imaginary wall and step forward and hit an imaginary ball.

BACK WALL RETURN

To practice the back wall return, stand facing the right (or left) side of a wall without a racquet. Position yourself in the middle of the court, about five feet from a back wall. Take the ball in your nonracquet hand and toss it against the back wall with an underhand motion. Toss it at your head height so it will bounce near your feet. Hold your racquet arm in the forehand position so the ball passes near your body without interference.

As the ball rebounds past you, slide your feet toward the front wall. Time this move with the descent of the ball so you can catch the ball (after it bounces) with your nonracquet hand just when the ball bounces to your knee height. This is the position you should use to hit the back wall return. Again, the practice drill is to toss the ball to the back wall, slide your feet, bend your knees and upper body as in the forehand stroke, and catch the ball with your nonracquet hand.

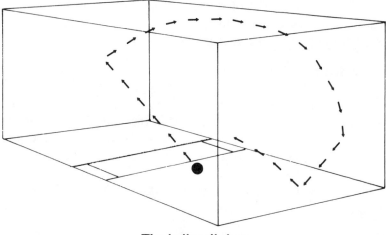

The ball wall shot

The back wall return

You should never toss the ball too hard, because it will fly by you. And never toss so that you do not have to move. Keep your sliding motion smooth, and do not cross your feet.

Now you are ready to use the racquet. Follow the same procedures as before, but now, instead of catching the ball in hand, strike it with the racquet. The ball should hit the front wall directly in a straight line with your body.

Back Wall Corner Return

Returning the back wall shot is one thing, but returning the back wall corner shot is another. In the corner you are at a disadvantage, and if you are able to return this ball, the return is usually weak and ineffective. Judging how a ball will bounce off two walls and the floor is very difficult to determine, yet you can practice and get some idea of the rebound direction simply by tossing the ball into the corner back wall area and observing its bounce.

There are two types of back wall corner returns.

(1) *Side-Wall Back-Wall.* The ball comes off the front wall to the floor, strikes the side wall, and rebounds off the back wall before it bounces a second time. This is the side-wall back-wall corner shot—the ball bounces before it goes into the corner. This ball must be returned before it strikes the floor a second time.

The basic mistake in attempting to return this ball is to follow the ball as it goes into the corner. If you do this, you end up with your back to the front wall, and from this position it is almost impossible to get the ball as it makes its rebound out of the corner area. Anticipating that the ball will hit the side wall near the corner, you will know it should rebound off the back wall to the deep center court. Thus, you move directly to the deep center court area to anticipate the rebound, keeping your back to the opposite corner. As the ball comes off the back wall, slide, as you do with the back wall return, into position to hit it as it comes to the right contact point.

Unlike the back wall return, which, after rebounding off the back wall goes straight to the front wall, the side-wall back-wall corner hit will angle toward the opposite side wall.

For practice, toss a ball to the side wall. As the ball rebounds off the back wall, let it bounce and slide with it. Let the ball drop to the proper forehand point, and then catch it with your nonracquet hand. Do this many times. Now use the racquet and attempt to return the ball, letting it bounce after coming out of the corner area. Your return should be a solid forehand stroke to the front wall.

Once you can return the side-wall back-wall shot after letting it bounce, try to strike it before it bounces to the floor.

(2) *Back-Wall Side-Wall.* The second back wall corner return is the back-wall side-wall. The ball bounces first, strikes the back wall, and then rebounds to the side wall. Practice this return as you would for the side-wall back-wall corner shot, except that when making the return it is not necessary to open up the leading foot as much—it will be more of a back wall return approach.

The key to success with both shots is knowing whether the ball is going to hit the side wall or the back wall first, and then quickly getting to the proper return area. You must judge the speed and angle of the ball as it comes out of the corner and let the ball drop to the proper contact point before hitting it.

BACK WALL HINTS

Whether you stop-and-hit or jog-and-hit, the prime rule is to follow the ball with your eyes and body so you are in a ready position. In the stop-and-start method, trail the ball back to the back wall, then stop and get ready as the ball strikes the rear wall. When the ball rebounds and arches toward the floor, step into it with a normal step, beginning with the left foot, followed by a right, and then a left step into the ball when hitting it. The rights and lefts are the opposite for backhands off the back wall.

If the ball rebounds off the wall with a hard shot, place yourself about four feet from the right side wall and three feet posterior to the service box. Give yourself a setup off the front wall to make the ball rebound moderately hard off the rear wall. The ball will carry toward forecourt. When the ball is going past your body from the forecourt side, shuffle after it toward the back wall, stop, and reverse direction in the position near the rear wall, and then step into the ball and smack it.

If the rebound is soft off the wall, the positioning is the same, except the ball will rapidly drop. Thus, retreat from the starting position to a stop (direction reversing), within three feet of the rear court wall. Then execute your shot.

GENERAL HINTS

1. When hitting the back-wall ball, remember that the proper point of contact for the forehand is out and away from your lead foot heel.

2. Fall back—side shuffle—far enough on back wall play. If you are too far forward, the ball will slice off the racquet strings and glance into the side wall.

3. Position yourself close enough to the back wall so that when you step into the swing, you do not move past the ball.

4. Step into the ball correctly in back wall play or you will lose points. You must be in the proper place for the rebound and have enough room to take a full swing.

5. Your body weight must be transferred from your rear to front foot during the stroke to ensure a correct downswing.

6. Watch the ball closely during play; as in tennis, this is vital.

7. Watch the ball when it hits your opponent's racquet, when it bounces, and when it rebounds.

11

Center-Court Strategy

Playing the court means playing as many balls as possible while conserving energy. Especially for the older player the strategy of covering the court is vital.

There is little sense in making racquetball a tough strenuous game—if you know how to hit the proper strokes and know your court and how to play it, the game will be a pleasurable and winning experience. I am sure you have seen players scurrying like mice on a court during a fast game. Don't play like that. There are ways to make the game come to you.

CENTER COURT

The importance of center-court position has already been discussed. When your movements are focused in center-court position, the game comes to you. If you can cover an area about fifteen feet behind the back service line and to within two feet of the side walls, you can retrieve rally shots into the back seven or eight feet of the court and cut off passing shots within two to three feet of the side walls. You will rarely venture into front court unless retrieving a weak shot by your opponent. Your offensive hitting range from the center-court position is what I am talking about.

THE FRONT WALL

Assuming you have a good center-court position, here are some tips to help you determine where the ball will travel after rebounding straight off the front wall without hitting a side wall—and how to handle the ball:

● An opponent's shot traveling at a reasonable speed striking the front wall no more than one foot off the floor will result in a ball falling into the front court.

● If the ball hits higher than a foot, but not higher than (say) two feet, and with good speed, the ball will bounce once and carry into or near center court area. You must cut off the ball here because if it gets past you it will die in deep court. Remember that any ball hit reasonably well and with speed in the target area will take a second bounce well beyond the service line. Don't make the mistake of moving into the service zone area for this ball. It will leave you wide open.

● When a ball hits high on the front wall (say) three feet, it will rebound at knee level so use a volley return. Don't back up to get the ball and don't allow the ball to get past you— it will draw you away from center-court position.

● A ball that hits high on the front wall (say) four feet or more is really welcome. Allow it to pass you and hit the back wall on one bounce or in the air. The ball will then rebound into the center court where you will be waiting for it.

PREPARING FOR A SHOT

Anticipating the shot and being ready for your opponents return is a natural part of most racquet sports. More so with racquetball. You want to reach as many balls as possible with enough time to set up properly.

Again, staying within the center-court area, start preparing for your next hit when you complete your follow-through stroke. Move to that center-court position where the ball is traveling and where your opponent is located.

As soon as the ball comes off your opponent's racquet, position yourself where you think the rebound will be—if you see a ball strike a side wall, stay near the middle of the center-court position because this is where the ball should rebound in that area.

In center-court position you will be taking one long step or stretch to reach a ball traveling along a side wall. Or you will be hitting a ball that is fairly close to your body.

Always keep your weight evenly distributed and your heels on the floor as you wait to see the direction of your opponent's shot. Most balls will come to you in center-court position with good velocity so be braced and ready. Keep your feet about two feet apart so you have a strong foundation when waiting for the ball. This position allows you to really stretch out or move toward a ball.

ANTICIPATION

Anticipating where your opponent's shot will land is a mental skill that comes with time. There are some hints to help you know where a ball might strike however.

● If your opponent is hitting off to one side, turn slightly so you can see the ball making contact with his racquet. Study the positioning of his body now—this will be the tipoff clue to just where that ball might land. If he is going to use a ceiling ball, his racquet will be traveling an upward arc.

● If he is looking to kill the ball or use a pass ball, the racquet head will be downward from its ready position around the head. Most players signal their shots with the position of the racquet. Disguising strokes is difficult and not many players can do it.

● While you cannot determine exactly *where* your opponent is going to hit the ball, you can anticipate *when* he is going to hit it so you can be ready. Footwork is another clue to where an opponent's shot might land. Watch your opponent's feet as well as his body position and his racquet swing. If this threefold observation technique seems difficult, it really is not. After a time you will do it routinely, but the main thing to learn is to do it.

GETTING CENTER-COURT POSITION

Remember that nobody owns the center-court position; it is always up for grabs depending on who has the best anticipation and the most accurate strokes. Both players have a right to the area. Generally, if you hit a ball down the sides of the court you will be able to stay in the center court and move into that area as your opponent runs to get your shot. But if you bring the ball to the middle you will have to move far enough to one side to allow your opponent sufficient room to hit. This does not mean you must vacate center court completely—move two to three feet away to the perimeter. When your opponent moves, get right back to the middle, unless of course his shot forces you elsewhere.

When possible, use kill shots into front corners or straight into the front wall. These shots when they rebound will force your opponent to the perimeter. A good pass shot will do this too. In either case, when your opponent goes to get the shot you will control center court.

Strike your passing shots low on the front wall to keep them from rebounding off the back wall and giving your opponent an easy set up.

Keep your position in center court by volleying every ball that comes your way in the air or about waist-level or below. If you let the ball go by you, a smart opponent will take over center-court control as you are forced into back court.

CENTER-COURT PSYCHOLOGY

Psych yourself to play center court as much as possible. Consider it the home base and always try to get back to it. After almost every shot try and return to the home base. If your opponent is already there, move in as close as good sense allows. Remember that although some shots down the side walls and into corners may elude you, in the long run it pays to stand right in the middle of that center-court position. This way you are playing percentages because most balls are going to come off the wall into the middle of the court—and to you.

For practice, tape an "X" directly in center-court and this will give you visual reference while playing a practice match with a friend. This will go a long way in teaching you how and where to position yourself for good racquetball play.

12

Doubles

Many people do not like doubles racquetball, but actually this is as exciting (with a proper partner) as singles play. A combined effort usually entails less physical exertion than singles play and for older people this might be desirable. And although it is true that the court seems crowded (actually, it is) with four players, I do not think this adds any hazard in doubles play.

Doubles play is, of course, somewhat different than singles play; one of the important aspects is picking a partner you can *play with*. Because doubles is a team game, it requires partners who coordinate well so they can both act quickly on the court without undue discussion. And the secret to good doubles play is to gain some experience playing with your partner. After a short time you will be able to determine if your partner is for you and vice versa.

FORMATIONS

The usual way to play doubles is the side-by-side or half-and-half court formation. Here each player is responsible for his side of the court with an imaginary line drawn down the center. Generally the player with the stronger backhand (assuming both are right-handed) takes the left side of the court.

A shot carrying down the middle of the court is the left-side player's responsibility because he is able to make a forehand shot on this. With a right and left team the half-and-half works even better, for both players are able to use their stronger forehand strokes the majority of the time.

Although there is an imaginary line down the center of the court, this is not a rigid barrier. For example, if the ball is coming down the center the left-side player would take it on the forehand (again, if both players are right-handed). But if the player on the left side is out of position, and this happens frequently, then the closer player makes the shot. As in singles, but more emphatically in doubles, control of the center court position is essential to successful games.

Another kind of doubles play is the I-formation sometimes called the front-and-back method. Here the imaginary line is drawn from side wall to side wall at about midcourt. The front player is responsible for shots in front of the short line and the other covers the backcourt. The ideal setup here is for the backcourt player to have a good defensive game and the front player to be able to shoot well from a deep-court position.

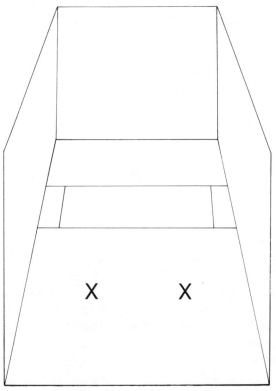

Side-by-side doubles position

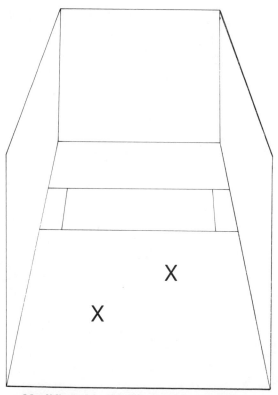

Modified side-by-side doubles position

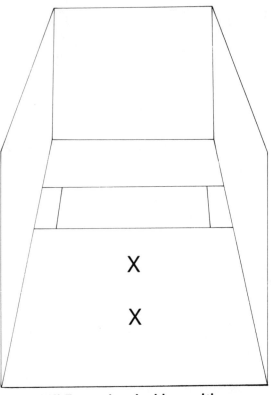

"I" Formation doubles position

SERVING

In doubles, the server takes a position in the service area in his half of the court. The partner stands in his service box in his half of the court. It is important to remember that neither player can move until the served ball has crossed the short line. If the first player serves and the team loses, service is then passed to the opposing team. If, however, the opposing team fails to win the point, the serve passes to the second member of that team. If the team loses a second point, the serve goes back to the first team. After that both players on each team continue to serve until the team loses.

To receive in doubles both players stand about five feet from the back wall and after the serve is returned both players advance to take center-court positions a few feet behind the short line. The objective in doubles is to get the ball in play deep to the back court so that the receivers are forced back. Then you and your partner get center-court position behind the short line. You can use a lob serve, a Z serve, or a drive serve.

The drive serve is probably riskier than the other serves because a hard hit ball can be returned offensively with more force.

MODUS OPERANDI

No matter what formation is used and what serve is made, the essential success of doubles is in getting center-court position.

With four players on the court be sure to watch the ball carefully and to know just where your partner is. Sounds difficult and it is. However, you must watch the ball to return it properly, and you must be alert to move if the ball is coming at you. You must also keep out of the way of your partner—bumping and clashing when you both run for the same ball is very possible. If necessary state your claim to the ball or, on the other hand, yell for your partner to get the shot if you see you are having trouble.

A good doubles game very much resembles a tightly staged ballet; once the teams have achieved mastery, it can make a beautiful bit of playing, especially if the partners have played together a bit and understand each other's techniques.

BASIC SHOTS

Service Return

If the serve is weak, realize that you can win the point by hitting a kill shot or a cross-court drive. Aim for a wide angle on the cross-court pass so that the ball cannot be touched by the opponents.

If the serve looks like it is going to be a strong one, it is best to go for the ceiling—then the return shot will be a tough one for your opponent to make. If you opt to hit the front wall, the ball may float up weakly to the wall and be easily reached on its rebound.

Pinch Shot

Passing shots are difficult in doubles because there is dual coverage. You really have to "power-pack" the ball to get the points in doubles. Thus, the pinch ball rebounding into the open court area is good strategy. Generally, your opponents are lagging back, playing defensively, so the pinch shot is tough to return.

The pinch shot is basically a kill shot: The ball angles low off the front wall and one side wall in either sequence. It is best hit within a two-foot range of the front corner.

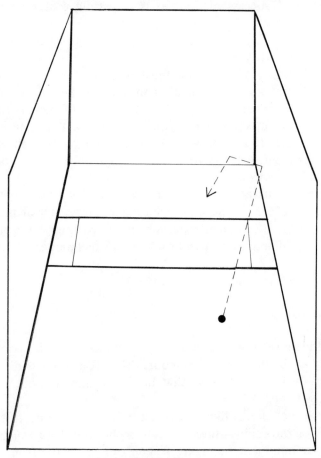

Pinch shot

The Volley

The volley will allow your team to hold a center-court position. In center-court position (in front of your opponents), you will have a greater chance to use an effective shot selection. With your opponents out of optimum-coverage position, a kill shot has a better chance of scoring and a cross-court shot makes for a difficult return.

Overhead Drive

The overhead drive and kill are just as effective in doubles as in singles. If the shot does not end the rally, at least it will force your opponents forward out of position. If the opponent is a little forward, try an overhead drive to force the ball to bounce high so it returns at his chest and makes for a difficult hit.

Ceiling Ball

Any time that your opponents' ceiling ball comes up short or goes long off the back wall, try to use a kill attempt or a passing shot. If the doubles game is becoming a ceiling ball rally, try an overhead kill or an overhead drive to change the game. Remember: the ceiling ball shot's basic purpose is to get your opponents out of the favorable center-court positions, and you do not want to risk a kill or pass attempt.

Center Court

Center-court position in singles is important—and in doubles vital. If you occupy center court, you can be in a better position for returns. You are also closer to the front wall and thus can be more accurate and powerful with your hits. Also it is much easier to see the ball if you are standing in front of your opponent.

13

Winning Tactics

In previous chapters we have discussed various shots and how to play them and now we explain in more depth when and why a certain shot should be selected.

STRAIGHT PASS SHOT

This shot rebounds off the front wall returning to an area where you were when you first hit the ball. This shot should be hit low enough so it is not playable off the back wall. The best time to use the straight pass shot is whenever your opponent is in the front-court area. When your opponent is to your left, the straight pass shot along the right side is a stellar choice, and even if your opponent is in the center of the court the straight pass shot can be effective.

CROSS-COURT PASS SHOT

This shot is generally good on return of service. As the server moves back to the attack position after his serve, the cross-court pass shot should be hit to angle toward the opposite deep corner after hitting the front wall. This puts your opponent out of the attack position in pursuit of the ball. The shot is best used when your opponent is in the front-court area. The closer he is to the front wall the less time he will have to get to the ball as it rebounds off the wall.

CEILING BALL

This ball is hit down the line or cross-court. In the down-the-line shot, the ball hugs the wall as it rebounds off the front wall; it is almost an impossible shot for your opponent to cut off well and forces him to return the ball from deep in the back court, which could result in a little or no real hit. The cross-court ceiling ball strikes the ceiling near the center very close to the front wall and rebounds into the opposite back corner of the court where your opponent will have little chance for a hit.

THE LOB

This is a floating shot to give you breathing time to get back into center-court position while it forces your opponent away from the center. Use the lob when you want to change the pace of the game and put pressure on your opponent.

THE KILL SHOT

This is the shot that hits low on the front wall and bounces off so it is unreturnable. Hit the ball low and hard about six inches from the floor so the return is too low for your opponent to make a shot. When you want to close out the point and have back-court position use the kill shot.

THE DROP SHOT

The drop shot is a controlled stroke with very little swing. You catch the ball on your racquet and push it gently toward the front wall. The change of pace of the drop shot can catch your opponent off guard, and he is hard put to get to the ball before it bounces twice. Use the drop shot when you are near the front wall and your opponent is farther back.

Z BALL

This shot can be hit with forehand or backhand stroke but you must be well behind the short line and quite close to one of the side walls. The ball hits the front wall hard near the opposite corner preferably high and near the side of the wall. The ball will rebound off the side wall near the corner and bounce cross-court deep to the opposite side wall where it will rebound into the court close to the back wall. This will force your opponent to be a whirling dervish to hit the wall, and if he does it will be a weak shot.

AROUND-THE-WALL BALL

This shot makes almost a complete circuit of the court and is hit to the opposite side wall first, near the corner and close to the ceiling. It then bounces off the front wall near the corner and goes cross-court to the opposite side wall, bouncing off close to the back wall. Use this shot when you are near the side wall midway in the court and your opponent is in front-court position.

MORE TACTICS

Player in Front, Opponent in Center Court

If your opponent is behind you in a game, try a kill shot to the front wall about six feet from the side wall. Your shot will rebound off the back court along the side wall where your opponent will have a difficult time returning it; at the same time it will draw your opponent out of center court.

Player in Back, Opponent in Center Court

Use a pass shot here to the opponent's weak side. Then you move to the center court quickly because the opponent must give up this area. If the pass shot does not move your opponent out of center court, try a ceiling shot and take center-court position.

The best time to use the *down the wall drive* pass is when the server is standing on the opposite side of the court from the receiver or when the server is moving toward the corner of the front wall of the court on the same side as the receiver. In either case this forces the server to give up the valuable center-court position, as he tries to return the ball.

From Back Court

If you are in back court, try the Z ball and overhead drive pass aimed across court or down the wall. Both of these shots will give you time to regain center-court position before the opponent can return the shot. The overhead pass works best when the opponent is in back court. If he is on the same side of the court as you, use a cross-court overhead pass shot. If he is on the opposite side of the court, a down the wall overhead pass is a good choice.

GENERAL GUIDELINES

It would be difficult to give *specific* plays for a player when his opponent is in certain areas of the court. I can only attempt to give some very *general* strategies here to help you. For example, let's study the kinds of shots you should use when your opponent is in different areas of the court.

Opponent in Front Court

- If you are also in the front court, then try a pass shot.

- If you are in the midcourt or back court hit a ceiling shot, Z ball, or around-the-wall return.

Opponent in Midcourt

- If you are in the front court, try a pass shot. The next best shots would be a pinch or Z ball.

- If you are also in midcourt, use a cross-court pass or a ceiling shot.

- If you are in the back court, try a cross-court pass, ceiling shot, or Z ball.

Opponent in Back Court

- If you are in front court, try a drop shot or a straight kill.

- If you are in mid-court, a good shot would be a straight kill or ceiling shot.

- If you are also in the back court, then use a front-wall side-wall kill or a ceiling shot.

Knowing Your Opponent's Modus Operandi

It is not easy to anticipate your opponent's shots especially if you play with different people frequently. However, there are some general guidelines to help you know *how he plays a game.*

- Does your opponent hit frequently into the backhand corner? When? Is there a pattern to his shots?

- After your opponent serves, does he move to center court or does he stay in the service zone?

- Is your opponent much more offensive with his forehand shots or with his backhand shots?

- On your opponent's service return, does he go to the nearest front corner or does he move down the sidewall when possible.

- When your opponent makes a cross-court shot does the ball hit the proper front wall angle or does it rebound off the side walls into the middle?

These are all questions that tell a great deal about your opponent's modus operandi—his weaknesses and his strong points.

Other Tactics

Can you "psych" out your opponent? Not really, but you can keep him on edge by studying him just before you serve—you will be able to determine whether he or she is leaning to one side or the other or "cheating" more to one side than another. Take advantage here and always serve to the weakness.

Just before you serve always glance at your opponent—this makes him aware that you know exactly where he is and gives you a better control of the situation. Indeed, the eye-to-eye contact can make an opponent somewhat nervous and this is what you are trying to accomplish without, of course, making yourself jittery.

Official Rules of the United States Racquetball Association

FOUR-WALL RULES

Part 1. The Game

Rule 1.1—Types of Games. Racquetball may be played by two or four players. When played by two it is called "singles"; when played by four, "doubles."

Rule 1.2—Description. Racquetball, as the name implies, is a competitive game in which a racquet is used to serve and return the ball.

Rule 1.3—Objective. The objective is to win each volley by serving or returning the ball so the opponent is unable to keep the ball in play. A serve or volley is won when a side is unable to return the ball before it touches the floor twice.

Rule 1.4—Points and Outs. Points are scored only by the serving side when it serves an ace or wins a volley. When the serving side loses a volley, it loses the serve. Losing the serve is called a "handout."

Rule 1.5—Game. A game is won by the side first scoring 21 points.

Rule 1.6—Match. A match is won by the side first winning two games.

Published by the United States Racquetball Association and National Racquetball Club. Reprinted by permission.

Part II. Court and Equipment

Rule 2.1—Court. The specifications for the standard four-wall racquetball court are:

(a) Dimension. The dimensions shall be 20 feet wide, 20 feet high, and 40 feet long, with back wall at least 12 feet high.

(b) Lines and Zones. Racquetball courts shall be divided and marked on the floors with 1½-inch-wide red or white lines as follows:

(1) Short Line. The short line is midway between and is parallel with the front and back walls dividing the court into equal front and back courts.

(2) Service Line. The service line is parallel with and located five feet in front of the short line.

(3) Service Zone. The service zone is the space between the outer edges of the short and service lines.

(4) Service Boxes. A service box is located at each end of the service zone by lines 18 inches from and parallel with each side wall.

(5) Receiving Lines. Five feet back of the short line, vertical lines shall be marked on each side wall extending three inches from the floor. See rule 4.7(a).

Rule 2.2—Ball Specifications. The specifications for the standard racquetball are:

(a) Official Ball. The official ball of the U.S.R.A. is the black Seamco 558; the official ball of the N.R.C. is the green Seamco 559; or any other racquetball deemed official by the U.S.R.A. or N.R.C. from time to time. The ball shall be 2¼ inches in diameter; weight approximately 1.40 ounces with the bounce at 68-72 inches from 100-inch drop at a temperature of 76 degrees F.

Rule 2.3—Ball Selection. A new ball shall be selected by the referee for use in each match in all tournaments. During a game the referee may, at his discretion or at the request of both players or teams, select another ball. Balls that are not round or which bounce erratically shall not be used.

Rule 2.4—Racquet. The official racquet will have a maximum head length of 11 inches and a width of 9 inches. These measurements are computed from the outer edge of the racquet head rims. The handle may not exceed 7 inches in length. Total length and width of the racquet may not exceed a total of 27 inches.

(a) The racquet must include a thong which must be securely wrapped on the player's wrist.

(b) The racquet frame may be made of any material, as long as it conforms to the above specifications.

(c) The strings of the racquet may be gut, monofilament, nylon, or metal.

Rule 2.5—Uniform. All parts of the uniform, consisting of shirt, shorts and socks, shall be clean, white or of bright colors. Warm-up pants and shirts, if worn in actual match play, shall also be white or of bright colors, but may be of any color if not used in match play. Only club insignia, name of club, name of racquetball organization, name of tournament, or name of sponsor may be on the uniform. Players may not play without shirts.

Part III. Officiating

Rule 3.1—Tournaments. All tournaments shall be managed by a committee or chairman, who shall designate the officials.

Rule 3.2—Officials. The officials shall include a referee and a scorer. Additional assistants and record keepers may be designated as desired.

Rule 3.3—Qualifications. Since the quality of the officiating often determines the success of each tournament, all officials shall be experienced or trained, and shall be thoroughly familiar with these rules and with the local playing conditions.

Rule 3.4—Rule Briefing. Before all tournaments, all officials and players shall be briefed on rules and on local court hinders or other regulations.

(a) **Pre-Match Duties.** Before each match commences, it shall be the duty of the referee to:

(1) Check on adequacy of preparation of the court with respect to cleanliness, lighting and temperature, and upon location of locker rooms, drinking fountains, etc.

(2) Check on availability and suitability of all materials necessary for the match, such as balls, towels, score cards, and pencils.

(3) Check readiness and qualifications of assisting officials.

(4) Explain court regulations to players and inspect the compliance of racquets with rules.

(5) Remind players to have an adequate supply of extra racquets and uniforms.

(6) Introduce players, toss coin, and signal start of first game.

(b) Decisions. During games the referee shall decide all questions that may arise in accordance with these rules. If there is body contact on the back swing, the player should call it quickly. This is the only call a player may make. On all questions involving judgment and on all questions not covered by these rules, the decision of the referee is final.

(c) Protests. Any decision not involving the judgment of the referee may on protest be decided by the chairman, if present, or his delegated representative.

(d) Forfeitures. A match may be forfeited by the referee when:

(1) Any player refuses to abide by the referee's decision, or engages in unsportsmanlike conduct.

(2) After warming, any player leaves the court without permission of the referee during a game.

(3) Any player for a singles match, or any team for a doubles match, fails to report to play. Normally, 20 minutes from the scheduled game time will be allowed before forfeiture. The tournament chairman may permit a longer delay if circumstances warrant such a decision.

(4) If both players for a singles, or both teams for doubles, fail to appear to play for consolation matches or other playoffs, they shall forfeit their ratings for future tournaments, and forfeit any trophies, medals, awards, or prize money.

Rule 3.5—(e) Referee's Technical. The referee is empowered, after giving due warning, to deduct one point from a contestant's or his team's total score when in the referee's sole judgment, the contestant during the course of the match is being overtly and deliberately abusive beyond a point of reason. The warning referred to will be called a "Technical Warning" and the actual invoking of this penalty is called a "Referee's Technical." If, after the technical is called against the abusing contestant and the play is not immediately confined within the allotted time provided for under the existing rules, the referee is empowered to forfeit the match in favor of the abusing contestant's opponent or opponents, as the case may be. The "Referee's Technical" can be invoked by the referee as many times during the course of a match as he deems necessary.

Rule 3.6—Scorers. The scorer shall keep a record of the progress of the game in the manner prescribed by the committee or chairman. As a minimum the progress record shall include the order of serves, outs, and points. The referee or scorer shall announce the score before each serve.

Rule 3.7—Record Keepers. In addition to the scorer, the committee may designate additional persons to keep more detailed records for statistical purposes of the progress of the game.

Rule 3.8—Linesmen. In any U.S.R.A. or N.R.C. sanctioned tournament match, linesmen may be designated in order to help decide appealed rulings. Two linesmen will be designated by the tournament chairman, and shall at the referee's signal either agree or disagree with the referee's ruling.

The official signal by a linesman to show agreement with the referee is "thumbs up." The official signal to show disagreement is "thumbs down." The official signal for no opinion is an "open palm down."

Both linesmen must disagree with the referee in order to reverse his ruling. If one linesman agrees and one linesman disagrees or has no opinion, the referee's call shall stand.

Rule 3.9—Appeals. In any U.S.R.A. or N.R.C. sanctioned tournament match using linesmen, a player or team may appeal certain calls by the referee. These calls are (1) kill shots (whether good or bad); (2) short serves; and (3) double-bounce pickups. At no time may a player or team appeal hinder, avoidable hinder, or technical foul calls.

The appeal must be directed to the referee, who will then request opinions from the linesmen. Any appeal made directly to a linesman by a player or team will be considered null and void, and forfeit any appeal rights for that player or team for that particular rally.

(a) Kill Shot Appeals. If the referee makes a call of "good" on a kill shot attempt which ends a particular rally, the loser of the rally may appeal the call, if he feels the shot was not good. If the appeal is successful and the referee's original call reversed, the player who originally lost the rally is declared winner of the rally and is entitled to every benefit under the rules as such, i.e., point and/or service.

If the referee makes a call of "bad" or "skip" on a kill shot attempt, he has ended the rally. The player against whom the call went has the right to appeal the call, if he feels the shot was good. If the appeal is successful and the referee's original call reversed, the player who originally lost the rally is declared winner of the rally and is entitled to every benefit under the rules as winner of a rally.

(b) Short Serve Appeals. If the referee makes a call of "short" on a serve that the server felt was good, the server may appeal the call. If his appeal is successful, the server is then entitled to two additional serves.

If the served ball was considered by the referee to be an ace serve to the crotch of the floor and side wall, and in his opinion there was absolutely no way for the receiver to return the serve, then a point shall be awarded to the server.

If the referee makes a "no call" on a particular serve (therefore making it a legal serve) but either player feels the serve was short, either player may appeal the call at the end of the rally. If the loser of the rally appeals and wins his appeal, then the situation reverts back to the point of service with the call becoming "short." If it was a first service, one more serve attempt is allowed. If the server already had one fault, this second fault would cause a side out.

(c) Double-bounce pick-up appeals. If the referee makes a call of "two bounces," thereby stopping play, the player against whom the call was made has the right of appeal, if he feels he retrieved the ball legally. If the appeal is upheld, the rally is replayed.

If the referee makes no call on a particular play during the course of a rally in which one player feels his opponent retrieved a ball on two or more bounces, the player feeling this way has the right of appeal. However, since the ball is in play, the player wishing to appeal must clearly motion to the referee and linesmen, thereby alerting them to the exact play which is being appealed. At the same time, the player appealing must continue to retrieve and play the rally.

If the appealing player should win the rally, no appeal is necessary. If he loses the rally, and his appeal is upheld, the call is reversed and the "good" retrieve by his opponent becomes a "double-bounce pick-up," making the appealing player the winner of the rally and entitled to all benefits thereof.

Rule 3.10. If at any time during the course of a match the referee is of the opinion that a player or team is deliberately abusing the right of appeal, by either repetitious appeals of obvious rulings, or as a means of unsportsmanlike conduct, the referee shall enforce the Technical Foul rule.

Part IV. Play Regulations

Rule 4.1—Serve (Generally).

(a) Order. The player or side winning the toss becomes the first server and starts the first game, and the third game, if any.

(b) Start. Games are started from anyplace in the service zone. No part of either foot may extend beyond either line of the service zone. Stepping on the line (but not beyond it) is permitted. Server must remain in the service zone until the served ball passes short line. Violations are called "foot faults."

(c) Manner. A serve is commenced by bouncing the ball to the floor in the service zone, and on the first bounce the ball is struck by the server's racquet so that it hits the front wall and on the rebound hits the floor back of the short line, either with or without touching one of the side walls.

(d) Readiness. Serves shall not be made until the receiving side is ready, or the referee has called play ball.

Rule 4.2—Serve-in Doubles.

(a) Server. At the beginning of each game in doubles, each side shall inform the referee of the order of service, which order shall be followed throughout the game. Only the first server serves the first time up and continues to serve first throughout the game. When the first server is out—the side is out. Thereafter both players on each side shall serve until a hand-out occurs. It is not necessary for the server to alternate serves to their opponents.

(b) Partner's Position. On each serve, the server's partner shall stand erect with his back to the side wall and with both feet on the floor within the service box, until the served ball passes the short line. Violations are called "foot faults."

Rule 4.3—Defective Serves. Defective serves are of three types resulting in penalties as follows:

(a) Dead Ball Serve. A dead ball serve results in no penalty and the server is given another serve without cancelling a prior illegal serve.

(b) Fault Serve. Two fault serves results in a hand-out.

(c) Out Serve. An out serve results in a hand-out.

Rule 4.4—Dead Ball Serve. Dead ball serves do not cancel any previous illegal serve. They occur when an otherwise legal serve:

(a) Hits Partner. Hits the server's partner on the fly on the rebound from the front wall while the server's partner is in the service box. Any serve that touches the floor before hitting the partner in the box is a short.

(b) Screen Balls. Passes too close to the server or the server's partner to obstruct the view of the returning side. Any serve passing behind the server's partner and the side wall is an automatic screen.

(c) Court Hinders. Hits any part of the court that under local rules is a dead ball.

Rule 4.5—Fault Serves. The following serves are faults, and any two in succession results in a hand-out:

(a) Foot Faults. A foot fault results:

(1) When the server leaves the service zone before the served ball passes the short line.

(2) When the server's partner leaves the service box before the served ball passes the short line.

(b) Short Serve. A short serve is any served ball that first hits the front wall and on the rebound hits the floor in front of the back edge of the short line, either with or without touching one side wall.

(c) Two-Side Serve. A two-side serve is any ball served that first hits the front wall and on the rebound hits two side walls on the fly.

(d) Ceiling Serve. A ceiling serve is any served ball that touches the ceiling after hitting the front wall, either with or without touching one side wall.

(e) **Long Serve**. A long serve is any served ball that first hits the front wall and rebounds to the back wall before touching the floor.

(f) **Out of Court Serve**. Any ball going out of the court on the serve.

Rule 4.6—Out Serves. Any one of the following serves results in a hand-out:

(a) **Bounces**. Bouncing the ball more than three times while in the service zone before striking the ball. A bounce is a drop or throw to the floor, followed by a catch. The ball may not be bounced anywhere but on the floor within the serve zone. Accidental dropping of the ball counts as one bounce.

(b) **Missed Ball**. Any attempt to strike the ball on the first bounce that results either in a total miss or in touching any part of the server's body other than his racquet.

(c) **Non-front Serve**. Any served ball that strikes the server's partner, or the ceiling, floor or side wall, before striking the front wall.

(d) **Touched Serve**. Any served ball that on the rebound from the front wall touches the server, or touches the server's partner, while any part of his body is out of the service box, or the server's partner intentionally catches the served ball on the fly.

(e) **Out-of-Order Serve**. In doubles, when either partner serves out of order.

(f) **Crotch Serve**. If the served ball hits the crotch in the front wall, it is considered the same as hitting the floor and is an out. A crotch serve into the back wall is good and in play.

Rule 4.7—Return of Serve.

(a) **Receiving Position**. The receiver or receivers must stand at least 5 feet back of the short line, as indicated by the 3-inch vertical line on each side wall, and cannot return the ball until it passes the short line. Any infraction results in a point for the server.

(b) **Defective Serve**. To eliminate any misunderstanding, the receiving side should not catch or touch a defectively served ball until called by the referee or it has touched the floor the second time.

(c) **Fly Return**. In making a fly return the receiver must end up with both feet back of the service zone. A violation by a receiver results in a point for the server.

Legal Return. After the ball is legally served, one of the players on the receiving side must strike the ball with his racquet either on the fly or after the first bounce and before the ball touches the floor the second time, to return the ball to the front wall either directly or after touching one or both side walls, the back wall or the ceiling, or any combination of those surfaces. A returned ball may not touch the floor before touching the front wall. (1) It is legal to return the ball by striking the ball into the back wall first, then hitting the front wall on the fly or after hitting the side wall or ceiling.

(e) Failure to Return. The failure to return a serve results in a point for the server.

Rule 4.8—Changes of Serve.

(a) Hand-out. A server is entitled to continue serving until:

(1) Out Serve. He makes an out serve under Rule 4.6, or

(2) Fault Serves. He makes two fault serves in succession under Rule 4.5, or

(3) Hits Partner. He hits his partner with an attempted return before the ball touches the floor the second time, or

(4) Return Failure. He or his partner fails to keep the ball in play by returning it as required by Rule 4.7(d), or

(5) Avoidable Hinder. He or his partner commits an avoidable hinder under Rule 4.11.

(b) Side-Out.

(1) In Singles. In singles, retiring the server retires the side.

(2) In Doubles. In doubles, the side is retired when both partners have been put out, except on the first serve as provided in Rule 4.2(a).

(c) Effect. When the server on the side loses the serve, the server or serving side shall become the receiver; and the receiving side, the server; and so alternately in all subsequent services of the game.

Rule 4.9—Volleys.

Each legal return after the serve is called a volley. Play during volleys shall be according to the following rules:

(a) One or Both Hands. Only the head of the racquet may be used at any time to return the ball. The ball must be hit with the racquet in one or both hands. Switching hands to hit a ball is an out. The use of any portion of the body is an out.

(b) One Touch. In attempting returns, the ball may be touched only once by one player or returning side. In doubles both partners may swing at, but only one may hit, the ball. Each violation of (a) or (b) results in a hand-out or point.

(c) Return Attempts.

(1) In Singles. In singles if a player swings at but misses the ball in play, the player may repeat his attempts to return the ball until it touches the floor the second time.

(2) In Doubles. In doubles if one player swings at but misses the ball in play, and in his or his partner's attempt again to play the ball there is an unintentional interference by an opponent, it shall be a hinder. (See Rule 4.10.)

(d) Touching Ball. Except as provided in Rule 4.10(a), any touching of a ball before it touches the floor the second time by a player other than the one making a return is a point or out against the offending player.

(e) Out of Court Ball.

(1) After Return. Any ball returned to the front wall which on the rebound or on the first bounce goes into the gallery or through any opening in a side wall shall be declared dead and the serve replayed.

(2) No Return. Any ball not returned to the front wall, but which caroms off a player's racquet into the gallery or into any opening in a side wall either with or without touching the ceiling, side or back wall, shall be an out or point against the players failing to make the return.

(f) Dry Ball. During the game, and particularly on service, every effort should be made to keep the ball dry. Deliberate wetting shall result in an out. The ball may be inspected by the referee at any time during the game.

(g) Broken Ball. If there is a suspicion that a ball has broken on the serve or during a volley, play shall continue until the end of the volley. The referee or any player may request the ball be examined. If the referee decides the ball is broken or otherwise defective, a new ball shall be put into play and the point replayed.

(h) Play Stoppage.

(1) If a player loses a shoe or other equipment, or foreign objects enter the court, or any other outside interference occurs, the referee shall stop the play.

(2) If a player loses control of his racquet, time should be called after the point has been decided, provided the racquet does not strike an opponent or interfere with ensuing play.

Rule 4.10—Dead Ball Hinders. Hinders are of two types—"dead ball" and "avoidable." Dead ball hinders, described in this rule, result in the point being replayed. Avoidable hinders are described in Rule 4.11.

(a) Situations. When called by the referee, the following are dead ball hinders:

(1) **Court Hinders.** Hits any part of the court which under local rules is a dead ball.

(2) **Hitting Opponent.** Any returned ball that touches an opponent on the fly before it returns to the front wall.

(3) **Body Contact.** Any body contact with an opponent that interferes with seeing or returning the ball.

(4) **Screen Ball.** Any ball rebounding from the front wall close to the body of the player on the side which just returned the ball, to interfere with or prevent the returning side from seeing the ball. See Rule 4.4(b).

(5) **Straddle Ball.** A ball passing between the legs of a player on the side which just returned the ball, if there is no fair chance to see or return the ball.

(6) **Other Interference.** Any other unintentional interference which prevents an opponent from having a fair chance to see or return the ball.

(b) Effect. A call by the referee of a "hinder" stops the play and voids any situation following, such as the ball hitting a player. No player is authorized to call a hinder, except on the back swing, and such a call must be made immediately as provided in Rule 3.5(b).

(c) Avoidance. While making an attempt to return the ball, a player is entitled to a fair chance to see and return the ball. It is the duty of the side that has just served or returned the ball to move so that the receiving side may go straight to the ball and not be required to go around an opponent. The referee should be liberal in calling hinders to discourage any practice of playing the ball where an adversary cannot see it until too late. It is no excuse that the ball is "killed," unless in the opinion of the referee he couldn't return the ball. Hinders should be called without a claim by a player, especially in close plays and on game points.

(d) In Doubles. In doubles, both players on a side are entitled to a fair and unobstructed chance at the ball, and either one is entitled to a hinder even though it naturally would be his partner's ball and even though his partner may have attempted to play the ball or may already have missed it. It is not a hinder when one player hinders his partner.

Rule 4.11—Avoidable Hinders. An avoidable hinder results in an "out" or a point, depending upon whether the offender was serving or receiving.

(a) Failure to Move. Does not move sufficiently to allow opponent his shot.

(b) Blocking. Moves into a position effecting a block on the opponent about to return the ball, or in doubles, one partner moves in front of an opponent as his partner is returning the ball.

(c) Moving into Ball. Moves in the way and is struck by the ball just played by his opponent.

(d) Pushing. Deliberately pushing or shoving an opponent during a volley.

Rule 4.12—Rest Periods.

(a) Delays. Deliberate delay exceeding ten seconds by server or receiver shall result in an out or point against the offender.

(b) During Game. During a game each player in singles, or each side in doubles, either while serving or receiving, may request a "time out" for a towel, wiping glasses, change or adjustment. Each "time out" shall not exceed 30 seconds. No more than three "time outs" in a game shall be granted each singles player or each team in doubles.

(c) Injury. No time out shall be charged to a player who is injured during play. If an injured player is not able to resume play after total rests of 15 minutes, the match shall be awarded to the opponent or opponents. On any further injury to same player, the Commissioner, if present, or committee, after considering any available medical opinion, shall determine whether the injured player will be allowed to continue.

(d) Between Games. A five-minute rest period is allowed between the first and second games, and a 10-minute rest period between the second and third games. Players may leave the court between games, but must be on the court and ready to play at the expiration of the rest period.

(e) Postponed Games. Any games postponed by referee due to weather elements shall be resumed with the same score as when postponed.

Glossary

Ace. Legal serve that goes untouched by receiver. One point is scored.

Anterior. Toward the front wall.

Apex. Highest point in bounce of the ball.

Around-the-Wall Ball. Defensive shot that hits high on the side wall, then the front wall, then the other side wall before finally striking the floor at three-quarter court.

Avoidable Hinder. A hinder or interference, not necessarily intentional, which clearly hampers the continuance of a rally. Results in loss of serve or point.

Back Court. Court area behind the short line.

Backhand. Fundamental stroke hit on the side of the body opposite the hand with which one plays.

Backhand Corner. Area of the court where the side wall and back wall join on the same side as the player's backhand.

Backhand Grip. Position of gun hand on racquet when stroking the backhand.

Back-Into-Back Wall Shot. Ball that is driven into the rear wall and travels on the fly to the front wall.

Back Wall. The rear wall.

Back Wall Shot. Shot taken on the rebound from the back wall.

Bullseye. Specific target area on the front wall which must be hit for a proper serve to result.

Ceiling Ball. Defensive shot which strikes the ceiling, then the front wall and then rebounds to the floor with top spin into deep back court.

Ceiling Serve. Serve that hits the ceiling. If the ball contacts the ceiling first, it is a side out; if it hits the front wall prior to the ceiling, it is only a fault.

Center Court. Floor area of the court described as starting from the front short line and extending posterior to about five feet behind the short line.

Center-Court Control. Maintaining position in center court, thereby forcing one's opponent to retrieve and make shots in deep court.

Change-Up. A shot hit softer than normal to throw the opponent's timing off.

Choke. To move the grip on the racquet handle toward the head.

Closed Face. Racquet face tilted forward. May cause ball to skip into the floor on kill shots.

Corner Shot. A kill shot that hits at or near the front right or front left corner.

Court Hinder. Interference of a normal rally by an obstacle that deflects the ball.

Cross-Court Drive. A hard hit shot that strikes the front wall and passes the opponent on the opposite side from which the shot originated.

Crowding. Intimidating the opponent by playing too close. This is an avoidable hinder.

Dead Ball. Any ball that goes out of play or causes a hinder situation.

Defensive Position. Player's station in rear court. An undesirable area for an offensive shot or for controlling play.

Doubles. Racquetball game where two teams composed of two players each compete.

Down-the-Line Drive. A shot hit from near a side wall directly to the front wall and rebounding back along that same wall.

Down-the-Line Pass. Down-the-Line Drive.

Drive Serve. Hard hit service that strikes low on the front wall and rebounds to the right or left rear corner.

Drop Shot. A softly struck ball, aimed low into the front wall.

Error. To miss the return of an apparently playable ball.

Exchange. The termination of the rally which results in a point or side-out.

Fault. Illegal serve or other infraction of the serving rules.

Five-Foot Line. Painted line five feet posterior to the short line which dictates the Five-Foot Rule (below).

Five-Foot Rule. Safety regulation stating that the receiver must stand behind the Five-Foot Line when receiving the serve.

Floater. Shot mishit or struck with excessive backspin such that the ball drifts slowly toward the front wall.

Fly Ball. Shot played directly on the rebound from the front wall before it contacts the floor.

Follow-Through. Completion of the stroke after racquet contact.

Foot Fault. Illegal placement of a foot before or during the serve.

Forehand. Fundamental stroke hit on the same side of the body as the hand with which one plays.

Forehand Corner. Area of the court where the side wall and back wall join on the same side as the player's forehand.

Forehand Grip. Position of gun hand on racquet when stroking the forehand.

Four-Wall Racquetball. The most popular variety of the game where two side walls, and front and back wall, and a ceiling are used.

Front Court. Area of the court in front of the short line, including the service box.

Front Wall-First-Ceiling Ball. Defensive shot that strikes the front wall first, then the ceiling and then the floor.

Front Wall Kill. A kill shot that strikes and rebounds directly off the front wall.

Game. One racquetball contest of 21 points.

Garbage Serve. A half-speed service that presents itself to the receiver at shoulder height.

Grip. Manner in which the racquet is grasped for forehand or backhand strokes.

Half-and-Half. A doubles formation as strategy in which each player is responsible for his side of the court.

I-Formation. One means of dividing court responsibilities between two players of a doubles team.

Kill. Shot that hits low on the front wall and rebounds with little bounce.

Let. A fault, hinder, or similar interruption of play.

Live Ball. (1) Any ball in play. (2) A racquetball that bounces satisfactorily or one which bounces too high.

Lob. A serve (or sometimes defensive shot) that is directed softly, with a high arc.

Long Serve. Any serve that carries to the back wall on the fly (before striking the floor). This constitutes one serving fault.

Match. A complete racquetball contest consisting of best two out of three games to 21 points.

Out. Loss of service due to an illegal serve.

Overhead. Pass or kill shot that is struck over the head.

Pass Shot. Down-the-line or cross-court shot hit out of the opponent's reach.

Point. Unit of scoring. Only the server may score points.

Rally. Time during which the ball is in play.

Safety Hinder. Interruption of play when further action could result in injury. For example, a mercy ball or foreign object in the court.

Serve. Act of putting the ball into play. Service.

Server. Player who puts the ball into play.

Serve Return. The receiver's initial shot after the ball has been served.

Service Box. (1) The court area between the front and short lines from which the server initiates the serve. (2) Area where player of a doubles team must stand when his teammate is serving.

Service Line. The front line, parallel to and five feet anterior to the short line.

Short Line. Line halfway between and parallel to the front and back walls past which the served ball must carry before hitting the floor.

Side-by-Side. See Half-and-Half.

Side-Out. Loss of service with the server and receiver exchanging positions.

Singles. Racquetball game where two players compete, one against another.

Southpaw. A left-handed player. Lefty, portsider.

Time-Out. A legal (30 seconds or one minute) interruption in play called by one player or team.

Top Spin. Rotation of the ball hit with overspin.

Unavoidable Hinder. An interference of normal play brought about unintentionally or uncontrollably by the players, the court, the equipment.

V-Ball. Cross-court pass shot. V-Pass.

Volley. (1) See Rally. (2) To take the ball out of the air on the fly.

Wallpaper Ball. Shot that hugs a side wall so closely it is difficult to return.

Winner. A successful kill shot.

Wrist Snap. Anatomical flexion of the wrist on the forehand and extension on the backhand that occurs at the point of contact.

Z-Ball. This ball hits high up on the front wall in either corner, ricochets quickly into the near side wall, then travels to the opposite side wall before finally striking the floor.

For Further

Exploration

BOOKS

Complete Book of Racquetball, Steve Keeley, DBI Books, Northfield, IL 1976

The Racquetball Book, Steve Strandemo with Bill Bruns, Wallaby Books, Pocket Books, NY 1977

Racquetball, Bill Verner with Drew Skowrup, Mayfield Publishing Co., Palo Alto, CA 1977

40 Common Errors in Racquetball, Arthur Shay and Terry Fancher, Contemporary Books, Inc., Chicago, IL 1978

Off The Wall, Charles Brumfield and Jeffrey Bairstow, The Dial Press, NY 1978

MAGAZINES

National Racquetball Magazine, 4101 Dempster St., Skokie, IL 60076

Racquetball Magazine, P.O. Box 1016, Stillwater, OK 74074

ASSOCIATIONS

United States Racquetball Association (USRA)
   National Racquetball Club (NRC)
   4101 Dempster Street, Skokie, IL 60076

Index

About the Author

Jack Kramer is the author of more than fifty books on horticulture and other crafts, including *Easy Plants for Difficult Places, Indoor Gardens How-to-Build-It Book,* and *Hot Tubs.* His work has also appeared in *Women's Day, Architectural Digest,* and *House Beautiful.* He is a syndicated columnist for the *Los Angeles Times Mirror.*

Although *Beginner's Racquetball* is his first book on the subject, he has been an active enthusiast of the sport for many years. A native of Chicago, Kramer lives in Mill Valley, California.